# COUNTRY SAMPLERS

## By ZUELIA ANN HURT

### Illustrated by MARY ROBY

OXMOOR HOUSE, INC., BIRMINGHAM

*City and rural scenes of one person's Southern heritage
are depicted in this counted cross-stitch sampler. The
alphabet leads the way for an original verse composed
to describe the rules of the contest for which this work
was created.*

# CONTENTS

# PREFACE

This book, *Country Samplers*, was inspired by a "Southern Country Heritage Sampler Contest" held in 1979 by *Progressive Farmer Company*. Had this same contest been offered 150 years earlier, no doubt many of the entries would have looked similar to Susan Bushey's sampler, page 7. By comparison, its nineteenth-century elements contain the familiar casual country-type charm of the samplers presented in this book. The same elements important in the last century continue to be an influence on how we feel a sampler should look today. We still love borders—lots of them—alphabets, inscriptions, and familiar surroundings that tell our own story.

*The essence of country life is expressed in this sampler's saying "Happiness Is Being A Farmer." Familiar objects of harvest and land are viewed as though a giant window looks out onto the farm.*

# SAMPLERS: PAST AND PRESENT

## THE SAMPLER'S ILLUSTRIOUS HISTORY

The products and tools of craftsmanship in any trade—needlework not withstanding—tell the story of its history as much as does the written word. Society's taste, style, industrial development and technology, morals, historical events, discoveries, and economic conditions all have been recorded through the eye of the needle.

Samplers, in their broadest meaning, are a record of history; in fact, they are a unique record form. In days before printing, when the only books were laboriously handcopied, the only means of remembering newly learned stitches or needlework patterns was to work a sample on fabric. Thus recorded, the sampler was available for later reference when stitches and patterns were selected for decorations on clothing and household linens.

Samplers were the "how-to books" of earlier generations. The word "sampler" comes from the Latin word *exemplar* and the French *essamplaire*. Though it is possible that professional needleworkers produced some of the early samplers for sale, most were stitched by adult women for their own pattern books and for sharing with others. One's personal sampler evolved over a long period of time—it was finished whenever the fabric was filled. In its origins the sampler was not considered a needlework project but a realistic registry of one's needlework vocabulary.

The professional needleworkers were mostly men who drew designs and worked the elaborate silk and gilt textiles for royalty and members of the court. For women who found it necessary to earn their own living, sewing and embroidering were among the few respectable occupations.

Exactly when samplers first began is not really known. The earliest surviving example has been dated by experts between A.D. 200 and 500 and is from an ancient Peruvian culture. The next examples, believed to be dated between A.D. 400 and 500, are fragments found in Egyptian tombs. Though the entry date of samplers into Europe is not known, it is clear that by the sixteenth century samplers had become both a fashionable and essential activity in the British court. Placing a profusion of needlework on male and female costumes and throughout the household, such as on bed canopies and linens, and on window draperies, was one of the most obvious means of displaying one's wealth.

The development of printing in Germany just prior to the mid-fifteenth century played a crucial role in the history of needlework. Within the next one hundred years, numerous pattern books became available, though only the rich could afford to buy them. Manuscript illuminations, herbals, and woodcuts provided additional printed design inspiration.

Making an example of a motif allowed one to learn the stitches, decide on color progressions, and estimate yarn yardages. These were important to know in advance of using the pattern in a project, because materials were expensive, even for the wealthy.

An English sampler dated 1598 was found in 1960. It is the earliest known dated sampler. The practice of signing and dating samplers did not become fashionable until the first half of the seventeenth century, during the reign of Charles I of England.

Sometimes a collector or an antiques dealer knowledgeable in textiles can establish an approximate date of an undated sampler. To do this, one must research carefully the trends and technology through the ages and then analyze the composition and style of the motifs, stitches, colors, dyes, and types of yarns and fabrics used to create the needlework. Additionally, chemical tests of the fabric and yarn fibers can be performed.

The first samplers made in America were greatly influenced by the English styles of that time. Wives and brides-to-be brought their samplers with them to the New World.

Among the first to be stitched in Colonial America was one by Loara, the daughter of the pilgrim, Captain Miles Standish. Dated to have been worked somewhere between 1633 and 1640, her sampler was of embroidered floral bands and a prayerful verse including her name.

A sampler by Anne Gower, circa 1610, was made in England and brought with her to America when she married Governor John Endicott of Massachusetts. It is considered to be the earliest sampler found in America. It is 8″ x 18″ and contains five cut and drawn whitework borders, an alphabet in flat whitework, and her name in white-eyelet stitches.

Whitework and blackwork were popular techniques for fifteenth- and sixteenth-century samplers. Frequently their shape was like a long narrow scroll. The embroidered scroll could easily be rolled up and put away, waiting for that next inspiring moment or social event, a time when women often exchanged patterns and ideas. Portability of needlework was as important then as it is today.

Spot samplers, those with motifs and stitches scattered at random over the fabric, and the band-style samplers, featuring horizontal motifs repeated across the narrow width of the fabric, were popular forms, even in America.

An excellent example of the band-style sampler can be seen on page 7 in Mary Pots's 1648 sampler. The band with three male boxers stands out among all the floral borders. These profile figures with one leg and arm extended were common motifs. The hand of the male is extended toward the female lover, shown here as a stylized female figure resembling a blossoming tree more than a lady. Older versions of the same theme contain realistic female figures.

The story-telling element, later to be so popular in America, was extremely rare in early samplers. Inscriptions began to be used during the middle of the seventeenth century. Gradually, the definition and purpose of samplers began to change from a record of work patterns to a teaching device or a display of accomplishments in needlework proficiency.

Much of this change in definition was due to the fact that America made the sampler a teaching tool in the female academies. Most of these schools were in the Northern states, which is why early school samplers from the South are rare. The average age of the young sampler maker was thirteen.

Some school samplers taught only stitch execution. They contained squares of darning and other sewing stitches, clearly intended to teach the student how to sew and repair clothing and household linens. Other samplers took on pictorial presentations displaying fancy embroidery stitches, the alphabet, a moralistic verse, the girl's name, the date, and, sometimes, the name of the school as well as the name of the teacher.

The teacher would draw the designs for the school samplers, and the students would copy them under her direction and stitch them under her supervision. Careful study of these samplers shows themes and subjects repeated regionally. In later years, it was not unusual for the former student to pick out the stitches of the last two numbers of the date in order to conceal her true age!

Early in the eighteenth century, American samplers began to take on their own identity. Borders were introduced into sampler making in 1721 by an eight-year-old girl, Mary Daintery. Although, by this time, the sampler was both a teaching device and a display piece, it is thought that this single element, the border,

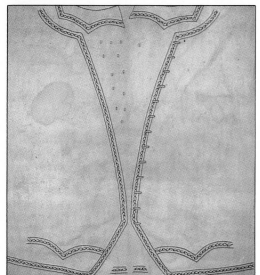

The cotton twill fabric in this eighteenth-century vest is embroidered with silk tambour work, which is a technique of forming chain stitches with a hook. The placement of the rosebud border clearly indicates the fabric was embroidered for a man's vest. Such a border would have been chosen from a sampler's selection of motifs. England, circa eighteenth century. (Author's collection).

*This American school sampler is signed and dated: ''By Susan Bushey February 1st 1838.'' Cross, stem, and satin stitches predominate the inscription: ''Methodist/E.P. Church St. Louis/Worked at E.B. Hms/School, Brunswick Chariton/County, Missouri.'' The Metropolitan Museum of Art, New York (Collection of Mrs. Lathrop Colgate Harper, Bequest, 1957). (57.122.756)*

*This is an English band-style sampler, much like the first examples produced in America. The bands are embroidered with colored silk on linen fabric in a variety of stitches; the upside-down inscription reads ''Mary Pots wrought this sampler and this date 1648''; 8" x 34½". The Metropolitan Museum of Art, New York (Rogers Fund, 1913). (13.109)*

did much to change the intention of the sampler from reference or study to one of display.

Memorial samplers are definitely an American innovation. The first ones appeared in 1799, commemorating the death of our first president, George Washington. Momentum for this style quickly spread as memorial samplers began to be used to express the loss of a family member, a sweetheart, or a public figure. Samplers became a way of recording the family's births and deaths—the family tree.

While the eighteenth century incorporated a great deal of freehand embroidery in crewel and silk yarns, the nineteenth century found a renewed interest for counted stitches. The execution was less fine and not as careful as in earlier years. Typically included were floral sprays, sentiments, geometric borders, scattered small motifs, and alphabets.

## PRESERVING SAMPLERS

Textile conservation must be considered as much a part of planning the new sampler as it is in preserving the antique example. Now is the time to start preserving your needleart in the best possible manner to elongate its life. It is not a disposable or temporary craft; it is made to be enjoyed and meant to be enjoyed for generations to come.

Light, both natural and artificial, is an enemy of all textiles. If an old sampler has become dry and brittle from long exposure, the best conservation may be to pack it away wrapped in washed muslin or acid-free tissue paper. If the item needs a stronger support for flat storage, add a piece of museum board (an acid-free mat board available from art-supply stores) or purchase an acid-free storage box.

Frame or mount pieces of needlework over museum board or wood which has either been finished with varnish or wrapped in washed muslin. Always avoid placing any textile directly against raw wood or any regular type of paper, because both are very acidic and will cause deterioration and discoloration. This also means that the inner edges of the wood frame which touch the front side of the needlework should be finished.

Protect the face of the framed sampler with a layer of glass or plexiglass that has been treated to cut out ultraviolet light rays. You may not wish to change the frame or glass on an antique piece; that would destroy its original value. In such cases you can add an extremely sheer layer of fabric over the needlework surface. Silk crepeline and malene veiling are excellent and are almost invisible to the eye.

Avoid tightly sealing the back of framed samplers. Place a breathable dust cover on the back made from muslin, canvas, or any open weave, natural-fiber fabric. This will keep the interior free not only from mildew but also from dryness.

Cleaning delicate old sampler surfaces can be a problem, one best handled by a professional, but should you wish to try on your own, then gather up a great deal of patience and a few tools.

Dust is a chief offender to old samplers. Enclose the edges of a piece of fine screen wire in tape. Place the screen over an area of the needlework, and with a small hand-held vacuum cleaner using low suction, proceed slowly and carefully over the entire surface of the screened area.

An alternate method of removing dust and powder from chenille yarns or sculptured stitches is to clean them very carefully with a sable brush.

Washing may be another cleaning option, but it should be done only by the professional textile conservationist.

## DECORATING WITH SAMPLERS

For most of us, needlework is a passionate avocation. We love making presents for others, for ourselves, for our homes.

In the truest tradition of sampler making, the projects displayed in the following room settings and clothing illustrations were all inspired by one or more elements from the thirty samplers presented in this book.

*Decorative and functional objects in a variety of materials—wood, metal, and china—combine dramatically with a collection of samplers for a wall that speaks country from ceiling to floor.*

The sampler's decorative touch is throughout this warm and wonderfully cozy dining room, **above,** inviting you to return after breakfast for a morning of stitching. **Above right:** Ginghams and solids are embroidered for the table linens. **Left:** The cross-stitched tab curtains resemble dish-towel linen when trimmed with ribbon stripes. **Right:** The cook's favorite apron is cross stitched with a pie safe. **MOTIFS: 117, 121, 131, 137, 140, 141, 146, 150, 157, 162, 200, 289, 338; 212, 305; 171, 179, 182, 185, 192; 324.**

**Left:** These country fashions are equally at home in casual city living. Blouse and split-skirt are both embroidered with trailing vines of brightly colored mixed flowers. The shirt's yoke and collar frame a simple arrangement of foliage with mums. **MOTIFS: 165, 167, 168; 170.**

**Below:** Visiting one's day-old colt deserves special attire. Pears, fences, and rainbows create yoke-shaped decorations on the cotton twill vest. **Above left:** A westward-bound wagon train is embroidered on the tote. **MOTIFS: 103, 214, 342, 349; 87, 90, 258.**

**Left:** *The farm couple portrayed in the two cross-stitch pillow-toys are just the right size for little folks. They and the soft-sculptured blocks, **below,** with A, B, C's and 1, 2, 3's await storytime and small loving hands.* **MOTIFS: 221, 222; 2.**

**Right:** *Home and hearth are never more inviting than when abundantly displayed with fine needlework. Above the mantel is a collection of samplers and barns, some in cross stitch, some freehand embroidery. The heart of hearts pillow, cross stitched on a woven check dress linen, has a double ruffle of ribbon and lace. The portrait pillow of home is made grand in scale by the large-count fabric on which it is stitched. Jumbo piping was shirred with bias baby gingham and applied to a perimeter which repeats the shape of the house.* **MOTIFS: 286; 75; 91; 111.**

**Above:** Nothing could be more country than all of your child's favorite farm animals assembled on a crib quilt. The center barn is banded by 10-inch squares with small animals, all in cross stitch. **MOTIFS: 11, 15, 24, 26, 33, 35, 74, 138, 190, 310.**

**Left:** This little piggy and friend are squealing for joy. A cross-stitched pig and trough are fenced in on this toddler's bib overalls; the waistband and pocket edges repeat the fencing detail. **MOTIFS: 4, 36, 74.**

# SAMPLER MAKING FROM A TO Z

## A PERFECT TEAM...
## INSPIRATION AND CREATIVE DECISIONS

**Inspiration and the basic decisions**

You have already had your first inspiration, that is to make a country sampler project. The following how-to chapters have been designed to encourage you to compose your exclusive sampler. The multitude of country motifs depicted can inspire you to do this. But, if you prefer, your sampler project can also duplicate any one of the illustrated samplers or sampler projects by putting together the prescribed combination of borders, motifs, alphabets, etc.

There are a few basic decisions to be made before starting on the stitching. Subject matter within the theme, functional or decorative usage, stitchery technique(s), fabric or canvas, yarn or floss, shape and size are all initial considerations.

Basic decisions can vary in importance from project to project. If where the finished project will be used is of uppermost importance, then size, shape, and color must be foremost considerations. Such is the case if there is a perfect spot for a small sampler in the bathroom, but it can be no wider than 7 inches when framed, and it must include colorful touches of coral and mint green to complement the towels and wallpaper. Those other decisions of length, subject matter, technique, and the physical materials will follow the dictated or primary needs.

While choosing the motifs and other elements for a sampler project, consider not only the basic needlework technique but also additional ones for details or main areas. Combin-

ing techniques, as many of our samplers do, can lend additional dimension and creativity to the project. For instance, an area could contain a motif worked on a contrasting fabric appliquéd onto the main fabric. Quilt batting can be layered under appliqués within needlepoint projects.

Most of the cross-stitch samplers utilize additional embroidery stitches for details. French knots for eyes, straight stitches for grass, and backstitches for outlining perimeters are typical examples. Some cross-stitch samplers utilize other stitches more boldly within the design. The "Yellow Seasons," pictured on page 47, although worked on Aida fabric for ease of the counted work, contains several motifs embroidered free hand without regard to the even-weave fabric. The sampler designed for the front jacket cover of this book exemplifies another use of multiple techniques. And on the needlepoint sampler, "School, Church, Barn, House," page 53, novelty stitches for trees and architecture form one dimensional effect while the surface-embroidered folks meandering throughout the landscape produce another form of relief.

The majority of samplers and other projects are worked in cross-stitch embroidery; but this should not hamper your creativity. The same cross-stitch charts can be executed in needlepoint stitches. The coded charts for counted cross stitch and needlepoint can be transposed into drawings suitable for freehand embroidery. And the drawings for embroidery can, likewise, be transposed into counted charts. A later chapter, "Great Tricks To Know," will explain how. But for now imagine all the expanded creative possibilities that can be included in your sampler by combining the forces of techniques and transposition.

**Inspiration beyond the frame**

When we think of samplers today, most often the image they take on will be in the form of framed pictures as decorative elements adding charm, warmth, and ambience to a room. But what can you do when all the wall space is filled and you are still trying to sustain a great passion for needlework?

Decorative and functional items can incorporate one or more individual motifs lifted from a sampler, expanding the country sampler's theme into a room full of coordinated country projects as already seen on pages 9–16 of this book.

Try something new! Needlepoint or hook a rug for the front hall or fireplace, embroider a canvas rug for the family room. Welcome baby with a sampler crib quilt, bib, hand-size learning blocks, cuddly pillow toys, or a soft-sculptured sampler mobile. Cover a footstool, the back of a wing chair, a window valance, or a fireplace screen with a charming country scene. Pad a box, picture album, desk blotter frame, and telephone book with coordinated country subjects. Decorate the kitchen sampler-style by embellishing tablecloths, placemats, chairpads, curtains, towels, tea-cozy and appliance covers.

The family's wardrobe can also be decorated. Embroider a child's crewneck sweater with a school house, put a westward-ho wagon on brother's jacket, a barn on dad's, and flower garden on mom's. Jeans, skirts, vests, overalls, shirts, and totes are all naturals for needlework display. Even canvas shoes look terrific decorated country style.

While every project is not in itself a sampler, it can be a sampler-inspired project in the true essence of what samplers historically were all about—recorded stitches and motifs providing inspiration for needlework needs. Any item that uses a textile can become a potential project.

# BEAUTIFUL FABRICS

There is such a large selection of fabrics and canvases today one could write an entire book on just that subject. The following selections include the most often used textiles for needlework projects plus a few original suggestions to enhance the country theme.

**Counted cross-stitch fabrics**

Counted cross stitch requires an even-weave fabric—a fabric that has been woven so that the number of yarn strands counted across within 1 inch is equal to the number counted down in 1 inch. In other words, the lengthwise and crosswise strands of the fabric have the same count.

The yarn counts within the multitude of even-weave fabrics vary from a very low number—a coarse weave, to a high number—a fine-weave fabric. Aida fabric, available in both a wide count and color range, is designed especially for counted cross stitch. The pattern within the weave forms squares separated by tiny holes. The needle is moved up and down through the holes to form crosses over the fabric blocks, thus producing stitches evenly spaced and of uniform size.

There are novelty even-weave fabrics, like Klostern with a slubbed yarn, which have texture or other distinguishing style characteristics even though the basic structure is similar to Aida's with blocks and holes. Gerda is an even-weave gingham, but if you don't mind a slightly elongated stitch, a regular dress gingham can be used successfully for counted cross stitch. The finer-count fabrics tend to have evenly spun yarns and can be used equally well for other counted embroidery techniques.

It is not always necessary to use an even-weave fabric for counted cross stitch. There is a special canvas, called waste canvas, available in a variety of mesh sizes. It is woven with a blue thread running at regular intervals lengthwise. A piece of waste canvas can be placed over any fashion fabric suitable for the project. It is cut large enough to accommodate the design area and then basted to the right side of the noneven-weave fabric. The cross stitching proceeds as usual over both the canvas and fabric layers. When the design is completed, the fabric and canvas are dampened in order to soften the starch in the canvas; then the canvas edges can easily be unraveled up to the stitches and pulled out from under the worked areas. If the base fabric is not washable, the canvas threads should be removed without dampening the fabric. Tweezers can help grasp the threads during the removal process.

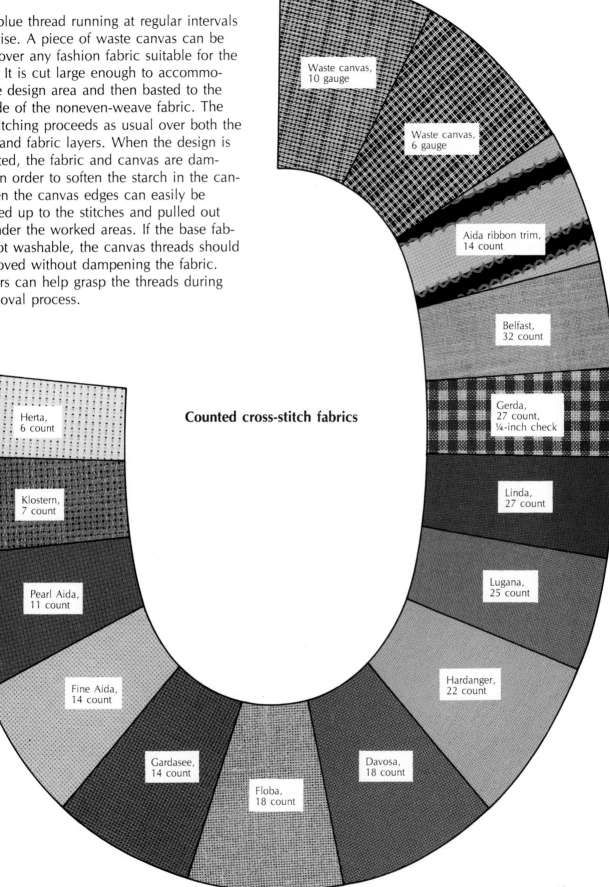

**Counted cross-stitch fabrics**

Waste canvas, 10 gauge

Waste canvas, 6 gauge

Aida ribbon trim, 14 count

Belfast, 32 count

Gerda, 27 count, ¼-inch check

Linda, 27 count

Lugana, 25 count

Hardanger, 22 count

Davosa, 18 count

Floba, 18 count

Gardasee, 14 count

Fine Aida, 14 count

Pearl Aida, 11 count

Klostern, 7 count

Herta, 6 count

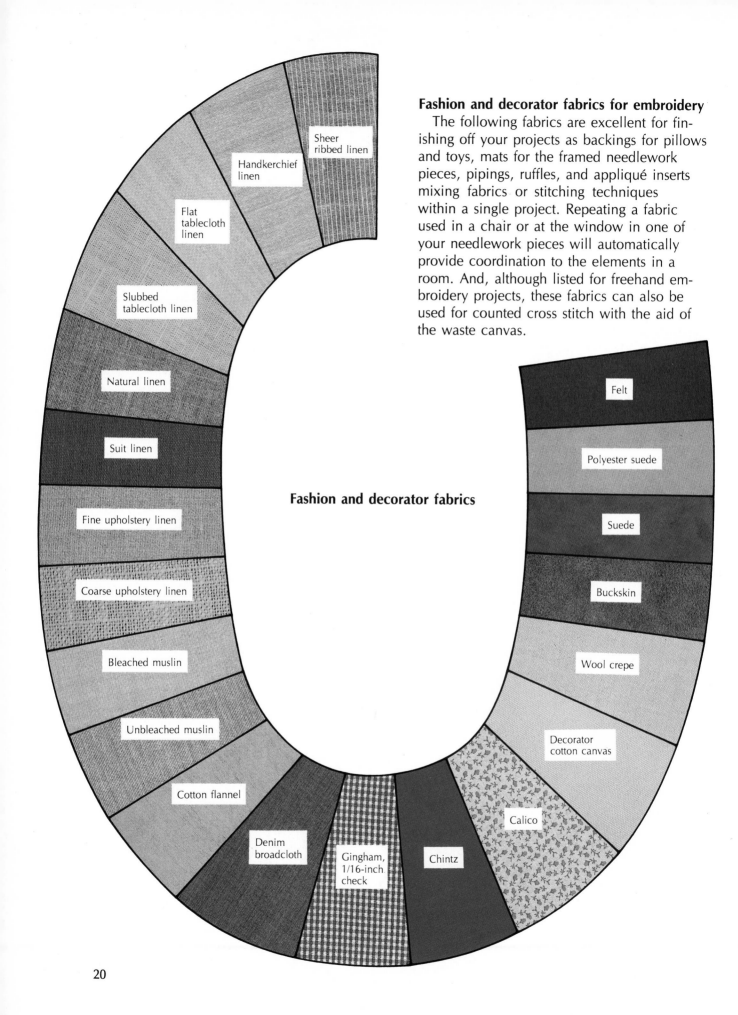

**Fashion and decorator fabrics for embroidery**
The following fabrics are excellent for finishing off your projects as backings for pillows and toys, mats for the framed needlework pieces, pipings, ruffles, and appliqué inserts mixing fabrics or stitching techniques within a single project. Repeating a fabric used in a chair or at the window in one of your needlework pieces will automatically provide coordination to the elements in a room. And, although listed for freehand embroidery projects, these fabrics can also be used for counted cross stitch with the aid of the waste canvas.

**Fashion and decorator fabrics**

Sheer ribbed linen

Handkerchief linen

Flat tablecloth linen

Slubbed tablecloth linen

Natural linen

Suit linen

Fine upholstery linen

Coarse upholstery linen

Bleached muslin

Unbleached muslin

Cotton flannel

Denim broadcloth

Gingham, 1/16-inch check

Chintz

Calico

Decorator cotton canvas

Wool crepe

Buckskin

Suede

Polyester suede

Felt

## Canvases for needlepoint

Needlepoint is also a counted technique. It is worked on an even-weave canvas. Woven canvases come in three types: mono canvas, mono-interlock, and penelope. Mono canvas is a regular plain-weave canvas. Mono-interlock canvas features pairs of lengthwise threads locked in a leno weave around each intersecting crosswise thread to prevent slippage or distortion of the grain. Penelope canvas is woven to one gauge which can be altered or doubled to become a gauge twice as fine by splitting the threads with the needle while working. Thus, the same canvas can contain needlepoint and petit-point stitches simultaneously without appliquéing a finer gauge canvas over the larger one.

When the whole surface of canvas is to be covered with needlework, mono-interlock or penelope is preferable. If part of the canvas is to be left visible, unworked, then a regular mono canvas is best since it has the appearance of a conventional even-weave fabric.

Each canvas type is available in a wide variety of gauges. Gauge refers to the scale of the canvas meshes, that is, the number of lengthwise/crosswise thread crossings per inch. The lower the gauge number, the fewer meshes, and the fewer stitches per inch.

Two of the canvases shown, plastic and woven vinyl, are washable, a desirable characteristic for some projects. Plastic canvas is a moulded grid available by the yard, in sheets, and in geometric, alphabet, and number shapes. Most plastic canvas is clear, but some sheets and shapes can be purchased in bold colors. Or, add color to clear plastic canvas by dyeing it in commercial home dyes.

The newest washable canvas is a woven vinyl that is heat set to stabilize the meshes together. It is available by the yard in several gauges and colors. It has the additional advantage of looking like a nice even-weave fabric, should you choose to cover only part of the canvas. It is also strong and pliable enough to be used for upholstery or sculptured shapes. Do make sure when using either type of washable canvas that the other materials to be used are also washable.

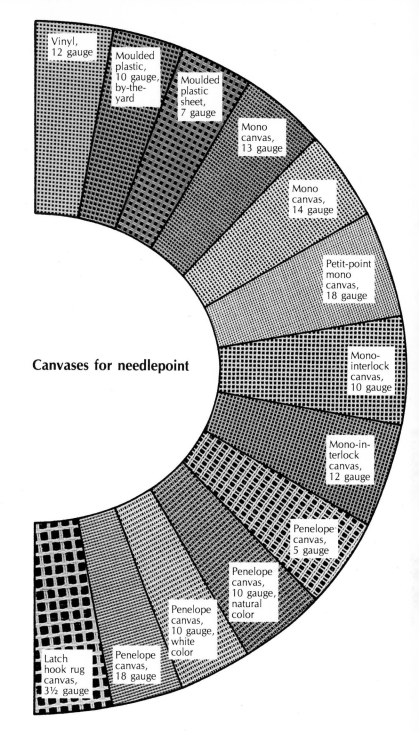

**Canvases for needlepoint**

Though we usually only think of canvas for needlepoint—tent or novelty stitches—it is also an excellent base for cross-stitch samplers. Choose the type of canvas based on whether or not you wish to fill in the background with stitches.

Most canvases are white in color. When painted in preparation for work, the design's colors remain bright and vivid. However, the older, traditional color of natural or beige is sometimes available and is pretty for country samplers when the background remains visible.

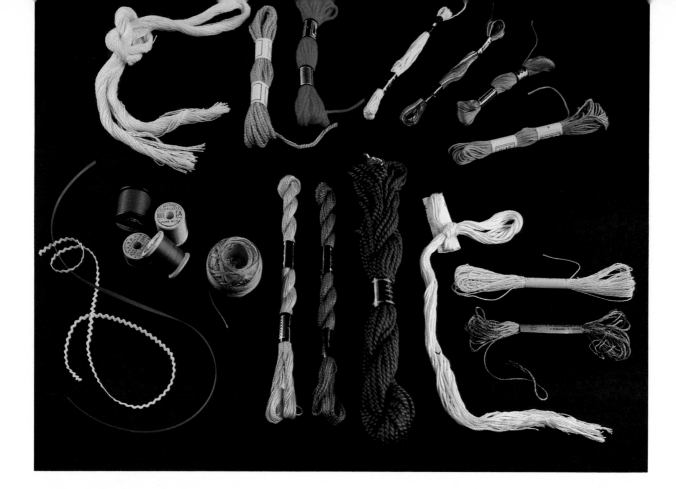

 # COLORFUL YARNS, FLOSS, AND THREADS

## THREADS

Select a yarn, floss, or thread that is appropriate to the type, weight, and care characteristic of the base fabric or canvas. Cross stitches, tent, and novelty needlepoint stitches should be worked with enough strands of the floss or yarn to give solid coverage over the base fabric. For freehand embroidery select a yarn size close to or slightly heavier than threads of the fabric.

### Yarns

Yarn differs from floss in that it is a plied strand meant to be used as it pulls out of the skein, ball, or cone. The exception to this is Persian yarn. Sometimes called 3-ply Persian, this yarn can be used with all plys together or separated into two 2-ply strands or one 2-ply.

Yarns can be made from cotton, linen, wool, metallic, or synthetic fibers. Yarns are spun to various weights or thicknesses and should be purchased according to the counted stitches being worked. The finer the base fabric, the finer the yarn will need to be. It is difficult to give a listing of yarn size for each size of a fabric or canvas, because the type of stitch being worked also influences the size of yarn needed. It is best to do some experimenting on your own to get a feel for what is the best combination.

### Floss

Floss is sold in skeins and constructed with multiple strands which can be used together as one strand, or the size of the floss can be adjusted by removing one or more strands. Additional strands from a separate length can be added to the first to add bulk to the size. Cotton floss contains six individual strands or threads loosely twisted together. Silk floss contains seven, and rayon contains four. Each fiber has its own personality, so experiment with those new to you.

### Threads plus

Threads, those very fine yarns usually used for sewing, can be used for extra-fine details or as cross stitches on a 25-, or finer, count

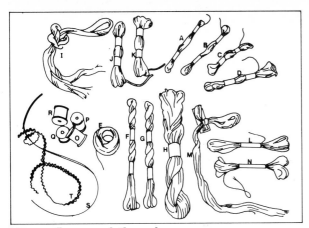

## Yarns, floss, and threads
A  Six-strand cotton embroidery floss, 6-ply
B  Variegated six-strand cotton embroidery floss, 6-ply
C  A Broder yarn (a fine, hard-twisted, single-ply cotton with sheen)
D  Retors A Broder yarn (or matte cotton, a medium-weight, hard-twisted, single-ply yarn with a dull finish)
E  Pearl cotton yarn, size #8 (extra-fine, single-ply cotton with a high sheen)
F  Pearl cotton yarn, size #5 (fine)
G  Pearl cotton yarn, size #3 (medium)
H  Pearl cotton yarn, size #1 (bulky)
I  Crewel wool yarn (extra fine with a hard twist)
J  Persian wool yarn (a three 2-ply softly twisted yarn)
K  Tapestry wool yarn (a plied wool, used singly, with a hard twist)
L  Linen yarn
M  Silk floss, 7-ply (medium sheen)
N  Rayon floss, 4-ply (high sheen)
O  Cotton sewing thread
P  Silk sewing thread
Q  Silk buttonhole twist
R  Polyester buttonhole twist
S  ⅛-inch wide satin ribbon*
T  Baby rickrack*

*Trims which can be used with yarns and threads for decorative stitches.*

fabric. Buttonhole twist, the silk or polyester variety, is slightly heavier and can be used for glossy highlights. Buttonhole twist is very nice when mixed with a dull yarn for random shiny spots.

While ribbons and rickrack are not technically yarns, the narrowest of widths can be used for decorative stitch accents or in combination with floss and yarn in couching or other laid stitches.

 # DECORATIVE TRIMS

### Pipings, ribbons, and laces
Pipings, ribbons, and laces add a special country flavor to sampler projects.

Use fine- to jumbo-size piping on the edges of pillows, between the mat and the framed sampler, or as a fashionable edge to your sampler-inspired wardrobe items. Stitch them in solid fabrics to match or contrast the item, or consider using a country calico print for a very special touch.

Ribbons of almost any width can be gathered and used singly or in various colored layers anywhere you want a ruffle. Gather and pleat ribbons quickly on the machine with an attachment. Ribbons can be more than just a pretty trim, they can add function, as seen in the tab curtains on page 10.

Laces—handmade or machine-made—are definitely a cozy country trim. Ecru Cluny lace and white eyelet are among the favored. Insert them, layer them, or gather them.

Eyelet edging, pregathered

Cluny lace edging, pregathered

Ball fringe

Loop fringe

Foldover bias tapes: calico, checks, dots

Large piping, selfmade

Regular piping, readymade

Rickrack: baby and jumbo

Rayon cording

Satin ribbon, single- and double-face

Grosgrain ribbon

*These decorative trims are available in a wide range of widths, sizes, and colors.*

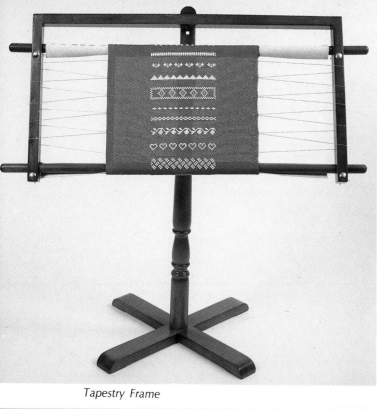

Tapestry Frame

Embroidery Hoop

*Larger grid drawn on separate paper to proportion will produce desired size increase; horse is duplicated on larger grid.*

*Final colored art of enlarged horse is ready for embroidery layout.*

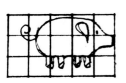

*Original drawing of pig shows grid lines drawn over motif in preparation for reduction.*

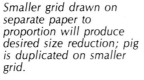

*Smaller grid drawn on separate paper to proportion will produce desired size reduction; pig is duplicated on smaller grid.*

*Final colored cut of reduced pig is ready for embroidery layout.*

## Forming mirror images

Some motifs may face in one direction when you wish to have them facing the opposite way for your layout, or you may wish to include both a right and left image of a motif in your sampler. Reversing the direction is a simple process. First, redraw the original chart of the motif on grid paper using colored pencils or pens. Place a small hand mirror on one side of the color motif, and duplicate the mirror image on a second piece of grid paper. It is important to use the mirror next to your color art and not directly by the charted motif

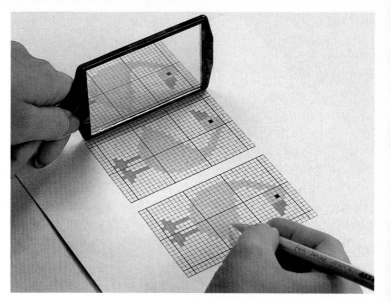

*Color art is drawn from charted motif, left, and reverse drawing is made from mirror image of color art, right.*

in the book. Placing it next to the coded chart in the book will become confusing since the code symbols will be altered by the mirror, changing the meaning of the color.

## Transposing coded charts into line drawings

Any of the coded charts for cross stitch and needlepoint can be transposed into linear art for freehand embroidery. After all, mixing techniques to show various stitches is part of the technical heritage of samplers.

If the size of the book's chart is what you want for the finished piece, you can start with the printed chart. Enlarge, reduce, or rechart the motif on a grid paper that will give the size you would like. Then place a piece of tracing paper over the printed or recharted motif. Using a pencil, draw the outer shape of the item and any interior details. Draw through the center of the symbols, and adjust the step-like stitches of the chart into curves

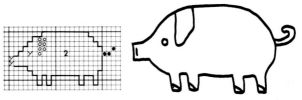

*Original coded chart of pig is left; chart is transposed into linear art for freehand embroidery, right.*

*Original coded chart for cloud is left; chart is transposed into linear art for freehand embroidery, right.*

*Final art is colored and ready for stitch interpretation and transference to fabric.*

appropriate to the shape of item being drawn.

Examine the examples of the pig and the cloud. Note how the chart shapes were adjusted to make the linear art more graceful and true to the image of the item.

Color-in the final art of the motifs to represent the yarn colors you wish to use in the sampler. Shading and other details can be added at this point.

**Transposing line drawings into charted art**

If a motif or sampler is presented as line art for freehand embroidery and you wish it to be charted for cross stitch or needlepoint, just follow these few steps of transposition.

Select a grid paper, preferably one printed on tracing paper, which is as close to the fabric count or needlepoint mesh as possible. If necessary, enlarge or reduce the linear motif photostatically or by hand as described on page 32. With the motif ready, place the line drawing under the transparent grid paper, and hold it securely with a piece of tape. Select colored pencils according to the yarn colors you wish to use in the motif. Fill in the

squares of the grid paper with color to represent the placement of the counted stitches.

If you cannot find transparent grid paper, then copy the line art motif onto a piece of tracing paper. Tape this motif on top of the regular grid paper, and tape a second clean sheet of tracing paper over the line art. You should be able to see both the line art and the grid lines through the top layer of tracing paper. Proceed with coloring the top paper following the shape of the squares and motif underneath. When the colored motif is complete, remove the line-art paper, and use rubber cement to glue the colored art on top of the grid paper.

**Adding appliqués to needlework projects**

Although these instructions are geared for adding appliqués into needlepoint, appliqués also can be added to other needlework by using this same technique. If you are appliquéing fabric onto fabric, it is not necessary to pad the appliqué with batting, but it can be a nice touch. Of course, if the added section is quilted, it will need the batting.

When appliquéing the fabric to a needlepoint sampler or project, first complete all the needlepoint areas, and block the piece, if

*Line drawing is placed under transparent grid paper with colored chart being started.*

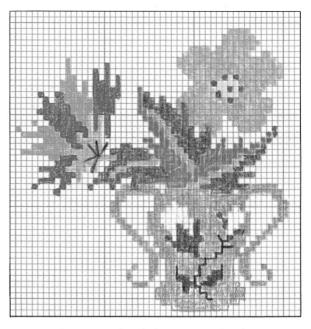

*Transposition onto colored chart is completed.*

necessary. Place a piece of plain paper over a cork or cardboard surface, and top with the needlepoint, right side up. Weight the layer/s with a heavy object to prevent slippage.

Next, following the perimeters of the areas to be appliquéd, prick around these shapes. Use a push pin or a hat pin. Remove the needlepoint. Use the pricked pattern to cut out the layer/s of batting or fleece—interfacing—enough to equal the depth of the stitches above the canvas. Draw your embroidery or quilting design on the same pricked pattern, and transfer it onto the fabric. Be sure to use a piece of fabric large enough to accommodate your hoop or frame.

For a quilted appliqué, baste the layer/s of batting in position under the fabric, and quilt as usual. For freehand embroidery, the batting can be added before or after working the embroidery stitches.

When the quilting or embroidery is completed, baste the batting to the fabric around the outside batting edge. Trim away the excess fabric, leaving ½ inch to turn under. If necessary, clip into the curves and corners of this fabric edge, being careful not to get too close to the outer basting line. Fold the seam edges in under, and pin or baste in place.

Baste the appliqué to the vacant spot on the needlepoint canvas. Use small invisible slip stitches, and hand sew the edge of the appliqué to the surrounding needlepoint stitches. Remove all of the basting threads, and finish the completed needlework piece in the planned fashion.

 # HEADING TOWARDS THE LAYOUT

## Charting and drawing the elements

Once you have decided on a sampler project and made the basic decisions on size, colors, materials, etc., you can start preparing the elements for the final layout.

If you are reproducing one of the book's samplers, make a list of the motif numbers included in that project. (You will find the list of numbers with the photography caption of the item on pages 44-56.)

If you are making a personalized country sampler, make a list of the motif and border numbers you like and want to include.

Using your list of borders and motifs, re-chart the coded charts onto your own grid paper with colored pencils and pens. Interject any color changes you want into this chart.

Planning a layout can take either of two directions—from the inside outward or from the outside inward.

When you do not have to worry about the finished size of a sampler, then you will probably want to arrange the elements starting with the inner parts and then add the outer border. That is the easiest direction in which to work. But if you are concerned about final size, start working from the outside inward.

Use a grid size which will be comfortable for you to read from while doing the needlework. The scale of the grid on your paper, in most cases, will be much larger than the scale of the final needlework. This is nothing to worry about. Just remember that one square on the grid paper represents one stitch on the even-weave fabric or canvas. And use this simple formula to calculate the size of any element in the sampler or the complete size of the needlework: divide the number of squares in the width of the chart by the thread count of the fabric or the gauge of the canvas.

Use the same formula for width and length calculations. If the motif measures 28 squares wide by 35 high and the fabric is a 14-count Aida, then the worked motif will measure 2 inches wide by 2½ inches high.

Chart each of the elements selected on a separate piece of grid paper, or on the same piece, just as long as they can be cut apart later for making the layout.

If the elements are line drawings, you can trace them from the book onto tracing paper or have them copied photostatically. If they need to be enlarged or reduced to equal the final size needed, then follow the instructions given on page 32.

If your sampler is to contain a mixture of counted and freehand embroidery, omit making the final art size of the freehand sections until all of the counted areas have been worked on the fabric or canvas. There is no need to enlarge or reduce these motifs twice—once for the layout and another for the final size. You can roughly calculate the space available for a freehand motif by using the above formula during the layout planning stages to assure that it will be appropriate in shape and size. It is necessary to have the freehand elements drawn to the final size, because this is the art used to transfer the motif onto the fabric for embroidery.

The examples used in this chapter and the next, "Inside the Layout," are from the sampler on the book jacket's front cover. It contains many of the tactics you will want to know—forming continuous borders, overlapping motifs, cutting and splicing motifs into new formations, mixing techniques, and including words, poems, or alphabets.

It is important when drawing colored charts from the book's coded charts to keep the motif in its "top up" position. Some motifs are turned on their sides and labeled "Top of Motif." Unless noted in this manner, always read the motif by holding the book in its normal reading position. An unwarranted turn of the book will cause the color-code symbol to change in its color meaning.

# INSIDE THE LAYOUT

Composing a layout from all the separate motifs and borders you have just drawn is very much like putting together a jigsaw puzzle. You will need grid paper, tracing paper,

scissors, transparent tape, rubber cement or a glue stick, a pencil, and a ruler.

In planning the reproduction samplers, you will find that the photograph might show some motifs overlapping in the final arrangement, but you have two pieces of art, two separate motif charts. You can choose to overlap these, as originally shown, by trimming away the excess paper from around the uppermost motif and glueing it over the other in the photographed position.

In your original composition you might like to experiment with overlapping one or more separate motifs to add depth or perspective to the composition. Some of this was done on the front jacket sampler. The tractor was moved farther away from the barn. In the lower scene the original motif had the house in the center. This arrangement interfered with the vase of flowers which needed a central location, so the house, fence, and trees were separated and reassembled; the fence was extended; and more flowers were added at the right to soften the end of the fence.

*Make a rough layout of a motif's rearrangement, and use this later within the larger complete rough blueprint of the sampler.*

For all needlework techniques prepare grid paper to receive the various sampler elements. For counted work, repeat the size grid used to reproduce the colored borders and motifs. Piece together several sheets with tape.

**Tolerance**

In preparation of the layout for counted techniques, use a pencil to draw the visible size of the sampler on the grid paper. (Remember, count off the grid squares to equal the number of fabric threads within the sampler.) Between this measurement and the outer edge of the worked area, there needs to be unworked space, some tolerance. The amount of tolerance needed depends on the use of the finished sampler. More tolerance is needed when the project will be sculptured or stuffed so that the design does not disappear around the sides of the item. For an example, refer to the cover sampler. A tolerance of ½ to ¾ of an inch was used.

Inside this square or rectangle, add another set of length and width lines representing the desired outer edge of the border. The space between these two lines equals the tolerance.

Add another set of lines to represent the inner edge of the border. The distance between the outer and inner border lines represents the depth of the border.

Check the border design, and decide if the center will be a stitch or between stitches. Select the border's center by determining the focal point of the design. If the center is a stitch, then draw center lines down the middle of the center squares in each direction on the grid paper. If the center is between two stitches, then draw the center lines between two rows of squares, over grid lines.

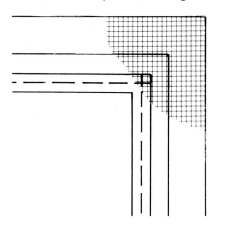

Though freehand-embroidery samplers do not need the grid paper for counting the stitches, it is, however, very helpful to use grid paper as the mounting paper for forming regular embroidery layouts. The grid lines can be thought of as fabric grainlines. They are useful in helping position borders in a straight line and placing other elements on the layout so that they will be on the fabric grainline.

For freehand-embroidery borders, add a broken line to the border's depth, and align the border's guideline over it when forming the final layout.

Before beginning the specifics of layout on the grid background, it is a good idea to first take all the elements involved and shuffle them around on the background grid to get various arrangement ideas. If you are reproducing one of the photographed samplers, this step will not be necessary. But if you are designing your own, this will give you some rough indication of size, shape, proportion, and whether or not all of the elements will fit into your original sampler composition.

Once you have selected the rough blueprint you like best, you can begin the final blueprint—the layout.

### Drawing and mounting outside border

Just because a border motif is drawn in one style—horizontal, vertical, or four-sided—does not mean you cannot change it to one of the other styles for your needs. Four-sided borders can be used in a single direction, and the single direction borders can be made to turn the corner. If the border has a complicated repeat, turning can be made easier by leaving space at the corner or adding a separate corner motif to join the sides.

### Charted borders

Examine the four-sided border shown on the jacket's front cover. This is an interesting example to analyze. It not only has a large repeat of 26 stitches in length—an even number—but also its focal point is a pair of flowers, each of which has an odd number of stitches. The border has a repeat depth of 15 stitches. The best visual presentation of this border is when either pair of flowers is centered over the center threads of the sampler.

This sampler had to fit within a specific measurement 8⅝ inches wide by 11¼ inches high—the visible size of the sampler.

Use the formula given on page 35 to calculate the size of a counted sampler according to the fabric's count or canvas's gauge.

If working on a 14-count fabric and the finished outside edge of the counted sampler should be no larger than 12 inches by 16 inches, you will have a maximum of 12 x 14 or 168 stitches in the width and 16 x 14 or 224 stitches in the length with which to work.

To fill this measurement exactly, the border repeat would have to fit evenly in both directions. In other words, the repeat size would have to divide evenly into the number of stitches on each side. In most cases this will not happen so easily and either the length or width will have to be slightly shorter or longer than this exact measurement. This is another important reason for planning on a generous tolerance area.

The easiest approach to planning a border is a visual one, thus avoiding most of the mathematics. On a large sheet of grid paper, reproduce the border repeatedly in color making it somewhat longer than the number of stitches required by the finished width of the sampler. Make a second piece of colored art for the length. The extra length included on each of these will come in handy while shifting the pieces around on the final layout.

Over the grid layout paper, hold the top repeat of the border so that the uppermost stitches are just under the top's outer edge line. Shift the row left or right until the center is in place. Hold the border row in place with a small piece of tape. Place the bottom border similarly in position on the grid.

Lay the side sections lengthwise inside the outer edge line. Examine the corners and how they come together. It may be necessary to shift the side rows left or right and the top and bottom rows up or down to arrive at a pleasing corner arrangement.

The corners can be handled in any of several ways: unjoined with open spaces between the sections; joined for a continuous flow of the repeat; joined with compensating stitches; joined with a corner motif.

Some borders may work best joined with compensating stitches added out of sync with the repeat. You must consider the border design and decide how easy or difficult it is to join the sides flowingly and still remain within the desired size specifications.

In the case of the example border, left, the decision was made to keep the seven repeats lengthwise. Reducing it to six would have increased the top and bottom tolerance areas disproportionately to the sides because of the size of the 26-stitch repeat. Leaving the seven repeats produced a tolerance of 6 threads at the top and bottom, a better proportion for the 8 threads tolerance on the sides.

Once the placement of the four sides and the corner methods has been established, the corners of the borders can be trimmed to follow this plan. If the border contains a corner motif, draw these on separate pieces of grid paper, and add them to the layout.

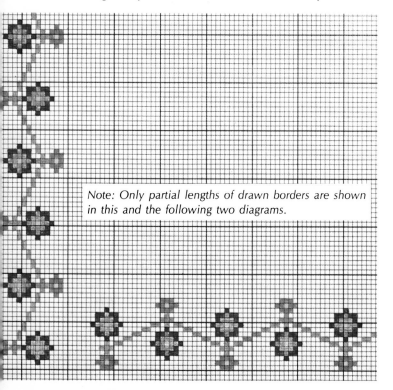

*Note: Only partial lengths of drawn borders are shown in this and the following two diagrams.*

*Width and length pieces of border are drawn repeatedly in color for preparation on layout.*

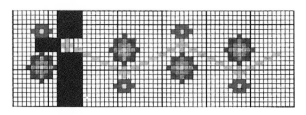

*Trim corners to join sides of border.*

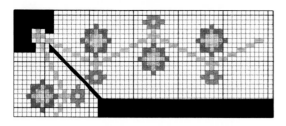

*With corners joined, glue border to layout.*

Join the corners of all sides, and glue the sections to the large background grid paper.

Once the border is glued in place on the layout, recheck the position of the pencil line representing the inner edge of the border on all four sides. This line will block off the inner area remaining for the sampler.

### Line-art borders

Drawing and placing line-art borders on a layout is similar to working with charted borders. The main difference is that the art must be drawn to the actual size of the final embroidery. This may necessitate enlarging or reducing the border motif to suit your needs, as described on page 38. The calculations for fitting in a given number of repeats will not involve the fabric's count or weave, just the length and depth of the repeat in relationship to the size available. You may choose to reduce the size/scale of a border in order to have a certain number of repeats fit in the length and width.

Repeating borders for freehand-embroidery samplers requires tracing paper, ruler, and pencil. You need to draw a perfectly straight continuation of the repeat. For each border piece, draw a guideline on a piece of tracing paper slightly longer than the length of border you need. On your copy of the freehand motif, draw a line through the middle of the repeat's length. Place the book copy under the tracing paper with the center line directly under the plumb line. Draw connecting repeats onto the tracing paper by shifting the repeat down each time while keeping the two lines aligned.

Make four pieces, two for the width and two for the length. You will have drawn a complete border for the layout that will eventually be the final art used to transfer the design onto fabric.

To arrange line-art borders for freehand embroidery on the layout, center a prominent detail over the center line of the background

*Line drawing of border repeated for border on sampler.*

layout grid, and center the line art inside the border area. Align the guideline on the drawing over the broken center border line. Examine how the corners are joined, and adjust the drawing, if necessary, to give a pleasing turn. Or, use any one of the methods for corner treatment suggested for counted charts.

### Mounting the inner elements

Trim away most of the excess grid paper from around each of the charted color motifs. If you wish to overlap two or more motifs into a group, trim the uppermost motifs next to the last row of color in areas where the underneath chart needs to be seen. Preferably, use

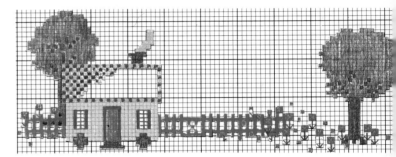

*Rearranged sections of the motif are mounted on a new piece of grid paper ready for application within the final layout for the sampler.*

rubber cement or a stick glue to layer the motifs. Transparent tape tends to diffuse the colors under it.

Glue the overlapping and singular motifs to the background grid paper following the rough pencil layout made on tracing paper.

When a single motif is being used repeatedly in a row, such as the garden vegetables on the jacket's back cover sampler, color enough separate motifs to fill at least half the row. Having the colored duplicates of the motif will also aid in figuring out the mathematics of how many spaces to leave between the duplicated motifs. Once the spacing is established, glue the left half of the row to the background grid paper.

When reproducing a sampler, sometimes you will find details such as fences that may be charted with some of the sampler's motifs and not with others, even though the photograph shows the detail continuing throughout various motifs of the sampler. You will need to superimpose the continuation of such details into your layout.

### Line-art motifs

Freehand-embroidery samplers made up of line-art motifs are prepared for layout similarly to charted designs. Either trace the motifs from the book onto tracing paper, or have them photocopied.

A few of the freehand-embroidery samplers have been left intact because the scenic nature of the designs could not easily be separated into motifs. These designs have been divided into units that will allow their actual size, or a slight reduction, to fit within the page size. To prepare these samplers for reproduction, all you need to do is trace the sampler's one or more units so that the entire scene is represented along with any border, or have the units photocopied.

If desired, enlarge the entire scenic sampler to its original size. This copy will become the art used to transfer the design onto the fabric by any one of the methods described in the following chapter, "Just Before You Start."

### Alphabets and verses

Chart any counted alphabet in color on grid paper. Do not worry about the arrangement of how the letters will break into rows.

Draw a linear alphabet on plain paper without concern of arrangement. Use a fine pencil line at the bottom to keep the letters level, and keep the spacing even between letters.

Draw any verse, date, or name to be included in charted or line-art form.

Mounting alphabets and numbers should be handled like motifs. Take the rows of letters and numbers which were drawn, and cut them apart to arrange row lengths which fit the layout. Glue the alphabet and/or verse rows together with the decided amount of blank grid rows or measured space between the copy rows. Use hearts or other small motifs and small borders to fill out short rows.

### Background details

The final inner details involve background stitches. Some background details in reproducing cross-stitch samplers will need your creative input on the final layout. "Milk

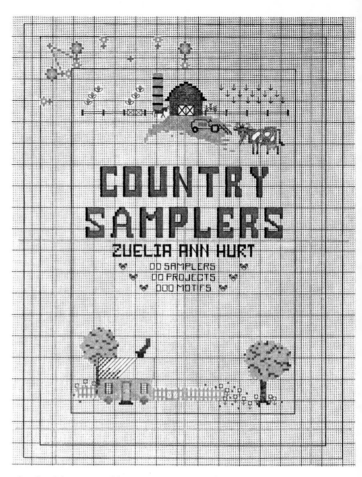

The final layout or blueprint is mounted and ready as a stitch reference for the needleworker. Note that the line-art motifs have been omitted from this larger than life-size charted layout. The line art will be prepared to the actual size of the embroidery after counted areas are stitched.

Drinkers" (photo on page 50) is a good example. The solid blue area behind the barn and farmer juts unevenly into the patchwork blocks of blue sky. In duplicating such an arrangement, glue the farmyard motifs into place across the layout, and with a pencil, draw a line above the scene representing the shape of the top on the light blue mountain range. Draw the line for such details in steps following the squares of the grid paper.

Grass and birds are other details which have been omitted from most motifs. You will find a variety of shapes and sizes within the appropriate subject section. Make a selection, and add them at random to the layout.

In adding background details to your own sampler composition, follow the same tactics as mentioned above.

It is always a nice finishing touch to include your name and the date of completion somewhere within the sampler. Some people also like to include the name of their city and state. That certainly would aid future historians and collectors in following the trends in twentieth century sampler-making!

Some needlepoint samplers need special handling of the background. Novelty stitches are sometimes used across the background, as in ''Apple for the Teacher,'' (photo on page 47). In such cases the various stitches are listed in their order of appearance, from top to bottom, along with the description by the sampler's photograph. Again, use your artistic judgment in defining the placement of these various background areas within the sampler and in determining the scale of the novelty stitch. This can be done easily by drawing in the novelty stitches on the background grid paper. Draw several repeats in the stitch's scale downward for the number of rows desired. Plotting the background out in this manner will eliminate many compensating stitches you might otherwise need between novelty stitches.

# JUST BEFORE YOU START

There are a few preparations to make on the fabric or canvas so the stitching will be neater, easier, and faster. Instructions follow for counted needlework, which includes counted cross-stitch and needlepoint stitches, and for freehand embroidery, which includes all noncounted stitches.

**Counted needlework**

Cut the fabric or canvas for counted needlework at least 3 inches larger on each side than the finished visual area. This tolerance measurement is a general one, basic to projects being made into pictures and pillows. The tolerance for other projects could be more. Less tolerance is not suggested because this amount is needed to fit the project adequately into a hoop or frame. For pictures the

tolerance will be needed when the sampler is mounted for framing.

To prevent raveling while fabric or canvas is being handled during work, stabilize the cut edges of the project in one of the following ways: stitch fabric edges on the sewing machine with a zigzag stitch, or encase the edges in a cotton bias foldover tape; bind canvas edges with masking tape, or stitch the edges inside a foldover tape.

For counted needlework it is important to

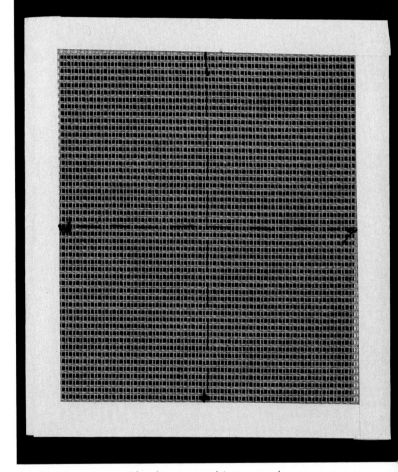

*Needlepoint canvas with edges encased in tape and centers basted is ready for work.*

mark the fabric or canvas with basting lines to denote the center length and width. If the center happens to be a thread or mesh (a stitch), baste a short diagonal line over this center thread/mesh. This type of center marking can be seen on the blue Aida fabric, in

41

*Fabric is prepared for counted needlework with diagonal bastings over center threads and the border placement marked with long and short bastings.*

the diagram above. If the centers are between 2 threads, mark them with long and short basting lines or stitches between the threads. When the design contains a border, it is helpful to baste the outer and inner placement lines. Use a long and short basting stitch, with the long stitch on the right side.

It is also possible to work counted cross-stitch embroidery on any fabric, even those

*Cotton flannel fabric has a waste-canvas grid basted on top in order to work counted embroidery stitches on a noneven-weave fabric.*

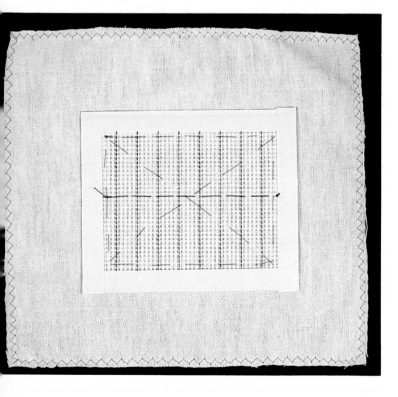

noneven-weave fabrics such as flannel, denim, gabardine, crepe, etc. Use a waste canvas over the desired base fabric. Cut and prepare the edges of the waste canvas as for needlepoint canvas, and baste the waste canvas grid over the base fabric. Work the design through both the canvas and fabric layers. When the work is complete, cut away the canvas to within an inch around the design, dampen the fabric and canvas to soften the structure, unravel the edges, and carefully pull out the threads from under the worked stitches. After all of the canvas threads are removed, all that will be left is the embroidery on the fabric.

**Freehand embroidery**

To prepare fabric for freehand embroidery, cut and stabilize the edges the same way as for counted fabric needlework. Within only the outer tolerance areas, make a short pencil mark denoting the center of each side. The marks will be helpful when mounting and stretching the finished sampler for framing or in sewing the work into a project. Be careful not to extend these marks within the final visual area.

In order to work freehand embroidery, the design must be marked or transferred onto the fabric in some manner. If the fabric is light in color, try pinning the final layout of the design under it and tracing the design onto the fabric with a sharp, hard-lead pencil, a fine-tip dry marking pen, or a wash-out pen (the lines disappear and dissolve in water). If the fabric is sheer, you might be able to see the design directly through the fabric. Otherwise, for tracing, you will need the aid of a light box or a lamp placed under a glass-top table. Or, tape the layers to a clean window pane, and let the sunshine aid you in tracing the design onto the fabric.

If the fabric is too opaque or dark for any of these tracing methods, try a transfer method. (First, make a quick test on a scrap piece of the same fabric to make sure the lines will transfer well, and keep the points of these pencils sharp at all times so the finest line possible will be produced.) You will need to draw the complete design in reverse with

*Opaque linen fabric is prepared with a scrim bearing the traced design basted on top ready for freehand embroidery.*

the transfer pencil, and then iron the transfer onto the fabric. Follow the instructions issued with transfer pencils, and practice on scraps before you begin.

Another technique for "transferring" the design to the fabric works without actually placing any marks on the fabric itself. The design is drawn onto a scrim of either silk organza or a sheer nonwoven scrim fabric. The scrim is basted to the right side of the sampler's fabric. The embroidery is worked through both the scrim and the under fabric. When the embroidery is complete, the scrim is easily trimmed away next to the stitches without a trace of the scrim being left. This scrim technique is best for designs with solid embroidery areas, because the remaining scrim would be visible under spaced stitches.

 # KALEIDOSCOPE OF STITCHES

All of the stitches used within the country samplers and the projects as well as the instructions on how to form them are presented in the Glossary of Stitches beginning on page 120.

It should be pointed out that many stitches can be worked in a variety of scales or sizes.

For instance, the popular cross stitch can be worked over one or more sets of intersecting fabric threads, thus producing a different scale of the stitch with each application.

On Aida fabric the cross stitch is worked over the prominent block of threads located between the prominent holes. On other even-weave fabrics and on mono needlepoint canvas, the cross stitch is worked directly over the intersection of one vertical and horizontal thread of the fabric or canvas.

However, on these same fabrics you can form a single cross stitch over a unit of four intersecting threads and produce stitches that are twice as large as the single stitch over the single intersection. It can be very interesting to incorporate more than one size of cross stitch within one sampler.

Penelope needlepoint canvas can be used the same way. This canvas is woven with pairs of threads in each direction. Form a cross stitch over pairs of threads for one scale of the stitch, or divide the pairs up into four individual intersections to produce four smaller stitches within the same space. In doing this, a 10-gauge penelope canvas becomes a 20-gauge petit-point canvas. Canvas gauges 18 and higher are placed in the petit-point category.

Needlepoint tent stitches can take on the same scale change as cross stitches. Some needlepoint stitches change their scale by continuing the length or rhythm of the stitch over more threads. The mosaic stitch, as an example, is worked diagonally over 1, 2, and 3 meshes and then returns to 2 and 1 in order to form the block of diagonal stitches. This type of stitch is easily increased in scale by continuing the rhythm past 3 to 4, 5, etc., and then reversing the sequence.

You will need to experiment on your charted motifs to decide which scale or stitch size is best for the size and shape of the motif and the fabric's count or canvas's gauge.

43

# LANDSCAPES... COUNTRY STYLE

The following thirty samplers were originally produced for the "Southern Country Living Heritage Sampler Contest" conducted in 1979 by the *Progressive Farmer* Company. Each one expresses a contemporary country story, life experience, and style and is an expression of America today.

The contestant's statements about their samplers were warm and personal—some are of memories past, some of present-day happenings. All the vivid stories told here are a continuation of America's history as told through the eye of the needle.

**Let Us Never Forget,** *9 by 11 inches. An embroidered sampler with bold six-strand cotton floss herringbone stitches used for the garden; the border and finer details use three strands of cotton or one of silk floss. All are on a fine off-white cotton fabric. The quote is from Daniel Webster. Motifs: 163, 170, 197, 347.* **Designed by Meg Tilley-Anderson, Georgia.**

**Make Mine Country,** *10½ by 16 inches. A cross-stitch sampler embroidered with one strand of cotton floss, using straight stitches, backstitches, and French knots for details, and worked on off-white Aida fabric (18 count). Motifs: 13, 16, 17, 22, 30, 40, 41, 49, 87, 90, 118, 121, 132, 141, 157, 172, 176, 177, 178, 183, 191, 193, 199, 200, 275.* **Designed by Marilyn Hutchinson, North Carolina.**

ABCDEFGHIJKLMNOPQRS
TUVWXYZ 1234567890
abcdefghijklmnopqrstuvwxyz
MAKE MINE COUNTRY
As ye sow, so shall ye reap
A swarm of bees in May is worth a load of hay
MARILYN HUTCHINSON 1980
far from bustling towns wide places
mountains, trees and boundless spaces

**All The Earth Is Full Of God's Glory,** *13¼ by 17½ inches. An embroidered sampler worked with two and three strands of cotton floss with counted cross stitches dispersed throughout for details on off-white Aida fabric (15 count). Motifs: 55, 58, 110, 113, 128, 168, 214, 277.* **Designed by Anita Westerfield, Georgia.**

**Fisherman's Farm,** *11 by 15¾ inches. A needlepoint sampler worked with Persian wool yarn, except for the silk-stitched fish and cow birds, on a 16-gauge canvas. Background stitches include U, M, FF, T, DD, and CC. Motifs: 8, 25, 28, 29, 48, 77, 138, 198, 220, 247, 262, 321, 327.* **Designed by Nancy Ann Brannon, Texas.**

**Yellow Seasons,** *9¾ by 14½ inches. This sampler, though basically cross stitch, contains several motifs embroidered without regard to the even-weave fabric with chain, satin, and turkey-work stitches. Two and three strands of cotton floss are used for most stitches; one strand for the fine backstitch details. All are on yellow Aida fabric (14 count). Motifs: 130, 140, 306, 349.* **Designed by Barbara D. Setzer, North Carolina.**

**Apple For The Teacher,** *11 by 16 inches. A needlepoint sampler worked with Persian wool yarn in a variety of novelty stitches on a 16-gauge canvas; background stitches include CC, AA, W, U, JJ, and V. Motifs: 5, 7, 79, 134, 136, 223, 300.* **Designed by Zana Mae Alldredge, Texas.**

**Draxie Kirby's Farm,** *9 by 7½ inches. A cross-stitch sampler embroidered in two strands of cotton floss using straight stitches, backstitches, and French knots for details, worked on cream-color Aida fabric (15 count). Motifs: 62, 98, 152, 186, 282, 331, 336.* **Designed by Draxie Kirby, North Carolina.**

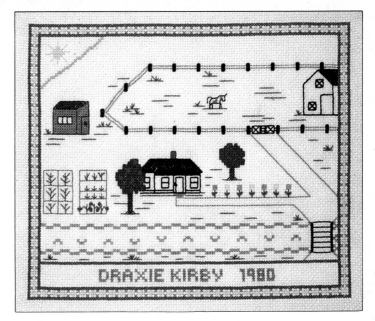

**Jan Morris's Rainbow,** *10 by 4¾ inches. A cross-stitch sampler embroidered with two strands of cotton floss, using straight stitches and backstitches for fine details, worked on cream-color Aida fabric (18 count). Motifs: 148, 268, 269, 284.* **Designed by Jan T. Morris, Mississippi.**

**Bradley Farm,** *14 by 10¾ inches. A cross-stitch sampler embroidered with two strands of cotton floss, using backstitches for the fence wire, and worked on ivory-color Aida fabric (14 count). Motifs: 33, 38, 53, 83, 102, 161, 237, 240, 242, 250, 272, 283, 292.* **Designed by Frances Bradley, Georgia.**

**Left: Goose Chasing Girl,** *11½ by 12 inches. An embroidered sampler worked with six strands of cotton floss on a dark, natural linen fabric and shown mounted on a firescreen. Motifs: 103, 104, 164.* **Designed by Farell H. Downey, Kentucky.**

**Far left: Thank You, God,** *13 by 16 inches. An embroidered sampler worked with one and two strands of cotton floss on a fine, white linen fabric. Motifs: 56, 59, 60 112, 114 165, 195, 196, 210, 211, 215, 216, 217, 278, 279.* **Designed by Carolyn B. Taylor, Tennessee.**

**Left: Milk Drinkers,** *12½ by 16 inches. This cross-stitch sampler gives the illusion of being needlepoint, with the background's highly stitched patchwork patterns for grass and sky. Three strands of cotton floss are used on off-white Aida fabric (12 count). Motifs: 31, 51, 100, 139, 206, 236, 238, 287, 291, 338.* **Designed by June O. Adams, West Virginia.**

**Falling Creek Farms,** *11½ by 19½ inches. A cross-stitch sampler embroidered with one strand of cotton floss, using the backstitch for fine line details, on off-white Hardanger fabric (22 count). Motifs: 12, 18, 26, 27, 36, 107, 119, 153, 160, 173, 184, 218, 243.* **Designed by Margaret S. Staley, North Carolina.**

**Far left: Mamie Poole's Poem,** *9 by 11 inches. A cross-stitch sampler embroidered with two strands of cotton floss, using several additional stitches for details on off-white Aida fabric (13 count). Motifs: 43, 80, 89, 96, 117, 131, 162, 244.* **Designed by Mamie Poole, Mississippi.**

**Left: Bobbi Rhea's Prayer,** *11 by 14½ inches. A cross-stitch sampler embroidered with two strands of cotton floss, using a block of four squares for one stitch on the house and trees and straight stitches and backstitches for details, worked on bone-color Aida fabric (18 count). Motifs: 6, 75, 94, 95, 126, 127, 150, 207, 255, 271, 333.* **Designed by Bobbi Rhea, Virginia.**

**Cotton Gin, House, Church,** *12¾ by 7¾ inches. A cross-stitch sampler embroidered with two strands of cotton floss on bone-color Aida fabric (12 count). Motifs: 73, 85, 106, 156, 158, 205, 263.* **Designed by Ann Geoghagan, Mississippi.**

**Ya'll Come,** *8¾ by 5 inches. A cross-stitch sampler embroidered with one strand of cotton floss, using straight stitches and backstitches for details, on cream-color Aida fabric (18 count). Motifs: 21, 50, 84, 145, 224, 273, 298, 316, 332.* **Designed by Jane Chandler, Georgia.**

**Blue Victorian Farm,** *11 by 9 inches. A cross-stitch sampler embroidered with two strands of cotton floss for crosses and one strand for the straight stitches, backstitches, running stitches, and French knots and worked on cream-color Aida fabric (14 count). Motifs: 37, 39, 68, 71, 81, 91, 99, 105, 155, 189, 225, 265.* **Designed by Debbie Daniels, South Carolina.**

**Country Life,** *10¼ by 15¼ inches. A needlepoint sampler worked with one strand of Persian wool on 13-gauge mono canvas. The horizontal bands of background colors incorporate a variety of stitches, from top to bottom—mosaic, Byzantine, Kalem, slanted Gobelin, diagonal mosaic, and tent stitches. Motifs: 10, 11, 86, 122, 208, 239, 249, 261, 274.* **Designed by Susan Weaver Crowder, Alabama.**

**Sylvia Rea's Farmyard,** *11¼ by 16 inches. A needlepoint sampler worked with Persian wool yarn in a variety of novelty stitches on a 14-gauge canvas; background stitches include JJ, T, V, Z, and A. Motifs: 32, 52, 67, 144, 180, 219, 253, 270.* **Designed by Sylvia Rea, Texas.**

**School, Church, Barn, House,** *15 by 28 inches. A needlepoint sampler worked with Persian wool yarn for the novelty stitched architecture and the background tent stitches, plus cotton floss for the folks embroidered on the needlepoint surface of a 14-gauge canvas. Motifs: 64, 70, 78, 97, 143, 227, 228, 229, 230, 231, 232, 251, 264.* **Designed by Mary Clark Barksdale, Alabama.**

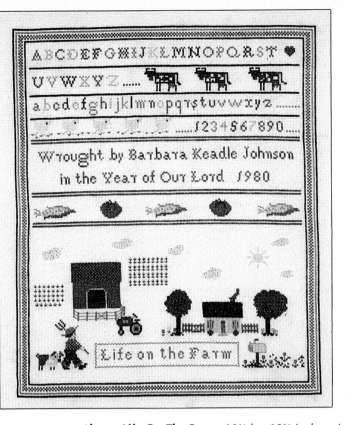

**Above: Life On The Farm,** *10½ by 12½ inches. A cross-stitch sampler embroidered with one strand of cotton floss, using backstitches, straight stitches, and French knots for details, on ivory-color Aida fabric (19 count). Motifs: 33, 42, 44, 74, 101, 129, 171, 182, 188, 190, 226, 248, 288, 308, 334, 335.* **Designed by Barbara Keadle Johnson, Georgia.**

**Above left: Home Sweet Home,** *11 by 11¾ inches. A cross-stitch sampler embroidered with two strands of cotton floss, using free-floating yarn under crosses for the barbed wire, worked on cream-color Aida fabric (15 count). Motifs: 19, 65, 88, 93, 120, 135.* **Designed by Peggy Taylor, Kentucky.**

**Jane Farrand's Alphabet,** *9½ by 11 inches. A cross-stitch sampler embroidered with two strands of cotton floss, using straight stitches and backstitches for details, on off-white Aida fabric (15 count). Motifs: 63, 82, 125, 133, 146, 260, 290, 319.* **Designed by Jane Farrand, Colorado.**

**Happiness Is Being A Farmer,** *9¼ by 9¾ inches. A cross-stitch sampler embroidered with two strands of cotton floss, using straight and backstitches for details, on off-white Aida fabric (14 count). Motifs: 15, 35, 69, 151, 159, 181, 187, 241, 245, 246, 252, 254.* **Designed by Beverly Gail Modlin, North Carolina.**

**Doris P. Scott,** *20 by 16 inches. An embroidered sampler, using a variety of stitches in two strands of cotton floss, on an off-white linen fabric. Motifs: 57, 61, 111, 115, 167, 169, 209, 235, 257, 259, 280, 281, 343, 346.* **Designed by Doris Scott, North Carolina.**

*Southern Country Living,* *10½ by 14½ inches. A cross-stitch sampler embroidered with two strands of cotton floss, using straight stitches, backstitches, and French knots for details, on off-white Aida fabric (12 count). Motifs: 23, 24, 66, 123, 137, 174, 175, 192, 202, 221, 222, 267, 285, 286, 289, 302, 329, 337.* **Designed by Mary E. Allen, Oklahoma.**

**Lindley's Mill,** *13½ by 13¼ inches. An embroidered sampler, using Persian wool yarn for all but the cotton floss stream of water, on a cream-color cotton fabric. Motifs: 108, 109, 166, 194, 344.* **Designed by Shirley Lindley, North Carolina.**

**Horse and River,** *4¾ by 4 inches. A miniature cross-stitch sampler embroidered with one strand of cotton floss on ivory-color Hardanger fabric (24 count). Motifs: 34, 72, 154, 276, 296.* **Designed by Kathryn Schade, Texas.**

**Farmhouse With Well,** *13¾ by 9⅜ inches. A cross-stitch sampler embroidered with two strands of cotton floss, using backstitches and straight stitches for details, on a light blue Aida fabric (15 count). Motifs: 54, 76, 92, 149, 299.* **Designed by Liz Runyan, Alabama.**

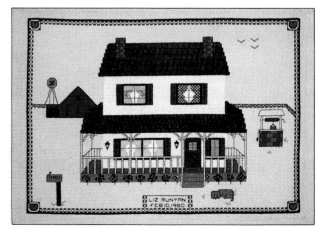

# MYRIAD OF COUNTRY MOTIFS

A brief description of the fabric, yarns, stitches, size, and listing of the sampler's motifs accompanies each photograph, along with the name of the needlewoman who designed the sampler.

To locate a specific motif by number, just look for it numerically in this chapter. To select motifs by subject, turn to the desired subject section, and make a selection from the variety available. For example, to choose a barn and a house for a sampler you are composing, look under the section "Architecture and Fences" and make a selection.

The country charts and drawings are numbered consecutively throughout the following eleven subject sections, "N" through "X". You may want to refer to pages 26-32 from time to time to review the specifics on reading the motifs. The color codes and stitch

codes are repeated below for your reference.

All of the line drawings appearing in the following subject sections are drawn the same size as they appear in the stitched sampler. If this is the size you desire, you need only trace the printed art to make a drawing for your layout. However, should you wish to enlarge or reduce the drawings, you will find the grey 1-inch grid lines helpful in making these adjustments, and the process is explained fully on pages 32-33.

Occasionally, a motif has been turned on its side in order for it to better fit the page. In such cases, you will need to turn the book in a direction so the label "Top of Motif" is upright, in the reading position. This will also insure an accurate reading of color symbols against their color representation in these motifs.

| Color Number Code | Color Name | Color Symbol Code |
|---|---|---|
| 1 | flesh | |
| 2 | black | |
| 3 | ivory | |
| 4 | white | |
| 5 | pink | |
| 6 | light yellow | |
| 7 | dark brown | |
| 8 | light tan | |
| 9 | light blue | |
| 10 | aqua | |
| 11 | beige | |
| 12 | hot pink | |
| 13 | light grey | |
| 14 | grey | |
| 15 | red | |
| 16 | brown | |
| 17 | gold | |
| 18 | lavender | |
| 19 | yellow | |
| 20 | rose | |
| 21 | purple | |
| 22 | orange | |
| 23 | green | |
| 24 | dark green | |
| 25 | cobalt | |
| 26 | peach | |
| 27 | light green | |
| 28 | blue | |
| 29 | rust | |
| 30 | dark tan | |
| 31 | dark red | |
| 32 | dark grey | |

| Alphabet Stitch Code | Name of Embroidery Stitch |
|---|---|
| A | cross stitch |
| B | straight stitch |
| C | satin stitch |
| D | backstitch |
| E | chain stitch |
| F | detached chain/lazy daisy stitch |
| G | long and short stitch |
| H | stem/outline stitch |
| I | French knot |
| J | herringbone stitch |
| K | turkey work (turkey tufting stitch) |
| L | running stitch |
| M | weaving stitch |
| N | buttonhole stitch |
| P | feather stitch |
| Q | wrapped straight stitch |
| R | couching stitch |
| S | bullion knot |
| T | tent stitches* (continental and basketweave) |
| U | mosaic stitch* |

| Alphabet Stitch Code | Name of Embroidery Stitch |
|---|---|
| V | upright cross stitch* |
| W | Kalem stitch* |
| X | straight Gobelin stitch* |
| Y | Florentine stitch* |
| Z | oblong cross with back-stitch* |
| AA | encroaching straight Gobelin stitch* |
| BB | leaf stitch* |
| CC | brick stitch* |
| DD | Byzantine stitch* |
| EE | slanted Gobelin stitch* |
| FF | diagonal mosaic stitch* |
| GG | double cross stitch* |
| HH | triangle stitch* |
| II | Jacquard stitch* |
| JJ | Hungarian stitch* |

*Indicates needlepoint stitches; all others are embroidery stitches. Note that the letter O is omitted to eliminate confusion with the number zero.*

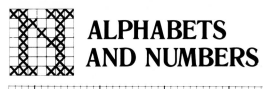

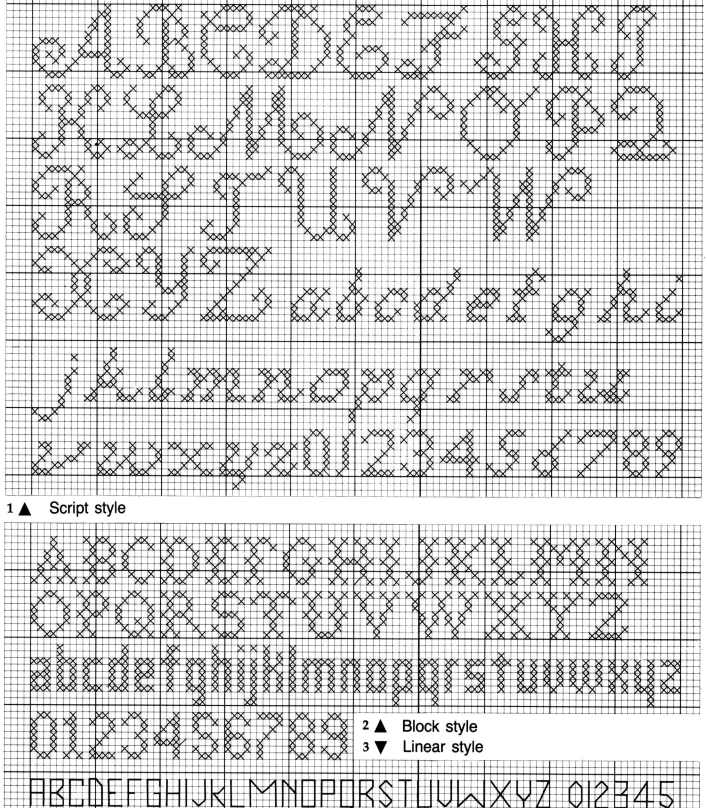

1 ▲  Script style

2 ▲  Block style
3 ▼  Linear style

ABCDEFGHIJKLMNOPQRSTUVWXYZ 012345
6789  abcdefghijklmnopqrstuvwxyz  0123456789

58

# ANIMALS

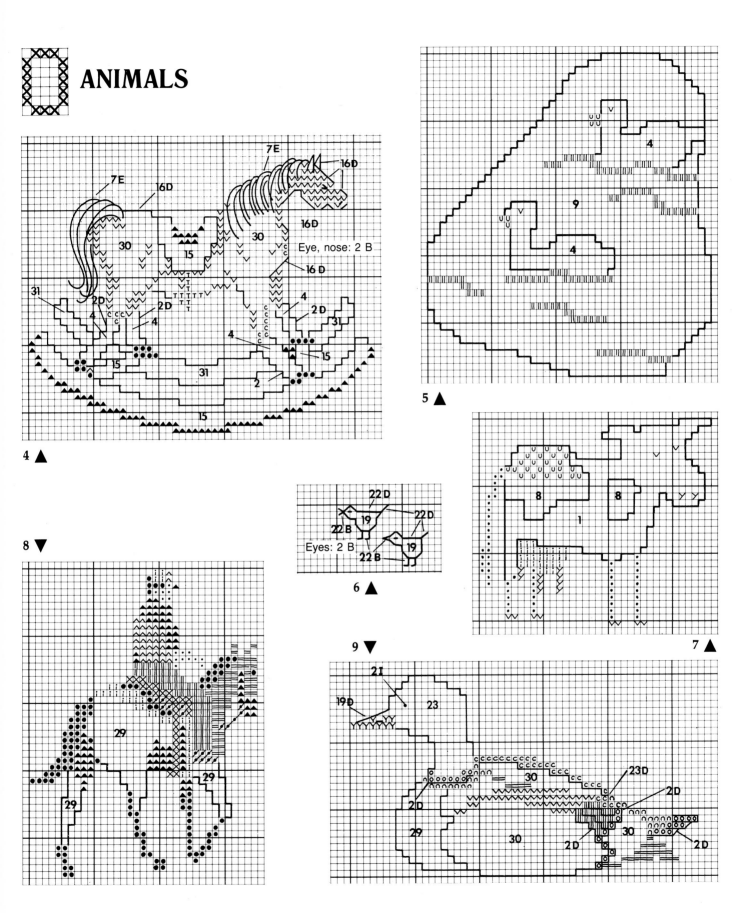

Eye, nose: 2 B

4 ▲

5 ▲

8 ▼

Eyes: 2 B

6 ▲

9 ▼

7 ▲

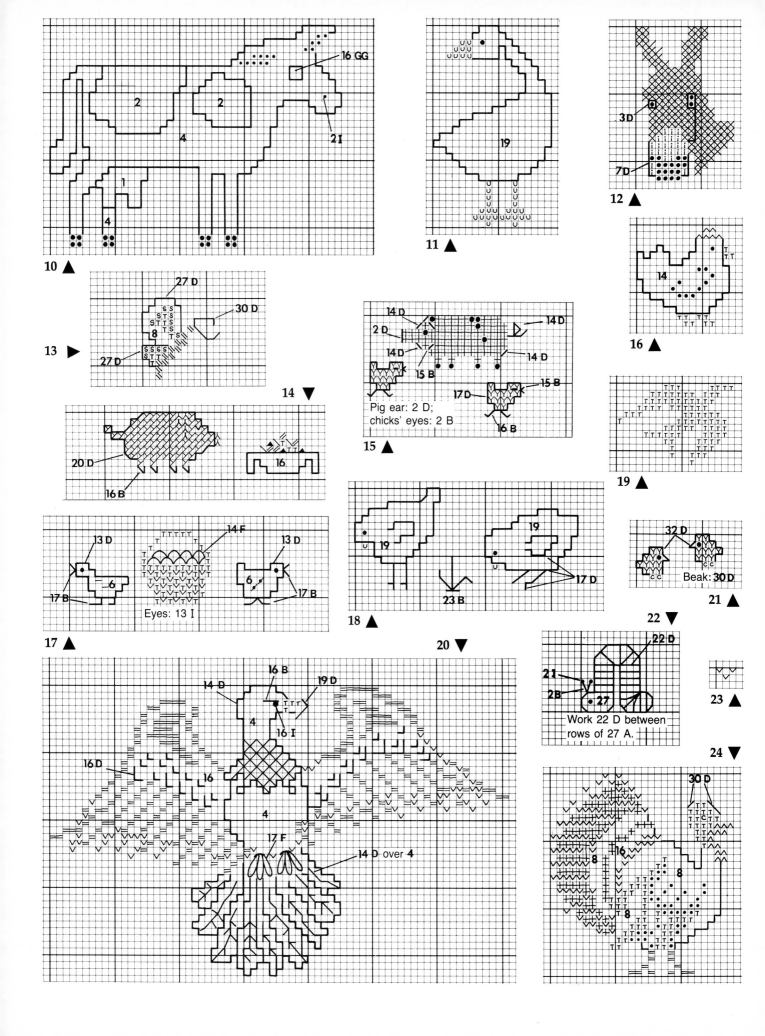

10 ▲

11 ▲

12 ▲

13 ▶

14 ▼

15 ▲

Pig ear: 2 D;
chicks' eyes: 2 B

16 ▲

17 ▲

Eyes: 13 I

18 ▲

19 ▲

20 ▼

21 ▲

Beak: 30 D

22 ▼

23 ▲

24 ▼

Work 22 D between
rows of 27 A.

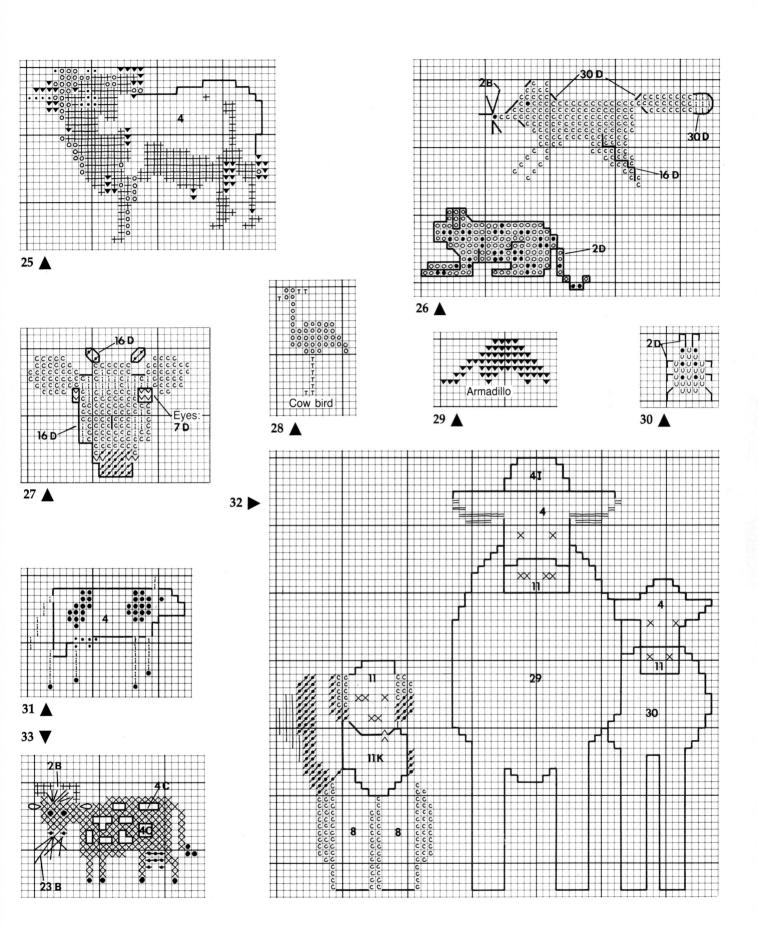

25 ▲

26 ▲

27 ▲

Cow bird

28 ▲

Armadillo

29 ▲

30 ▲

16 D

16 D

Eyes:
7 D

31 ▲

33 ▼

2 B

23 B

4 C

4 C

32 ▶

4 I

4

11

4

11

29

30

11 K

8    8

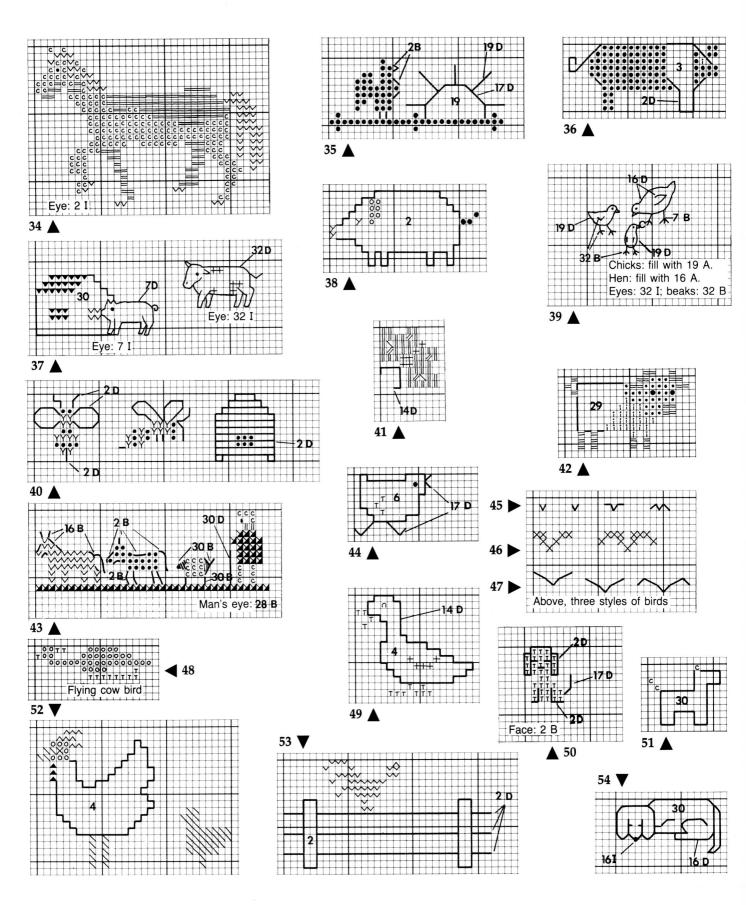

Eye: 2 I

34 ▲

32 D

30        7D

Eye: 32 I

Eye: 7 I

37 ▲

2 D

2 D        2 D

40 ▲

16 B        2 B

30 D

30 B

2 B        30 B

Man's eye: 28 B

43 ▲

48 ◄

Flying cow bird

52 ▼

4

2B        19 D

17 D

19

35 ▲

2

38 ▲

3

2D

36 ▲

16 D

19 D        7 B

32 B        19 D

Chicks: fill with 19 A.
Hen: fill with 16 A.
Eyes: 32 I; beaks: 32 B

39 ▲

14 D

41 ▲

29

42 ▲

6        17 D

44 ▲

14 D

4

49 ▲

45 ►

46 ►

47 ►

Above, three styles of birds

2 D

17 D

2 D

Face: 2 B

▲ 50

c c
c        c
30

51 ▲

54 ▼

30

16 I        16 D

2 D

2

53 ▼

62

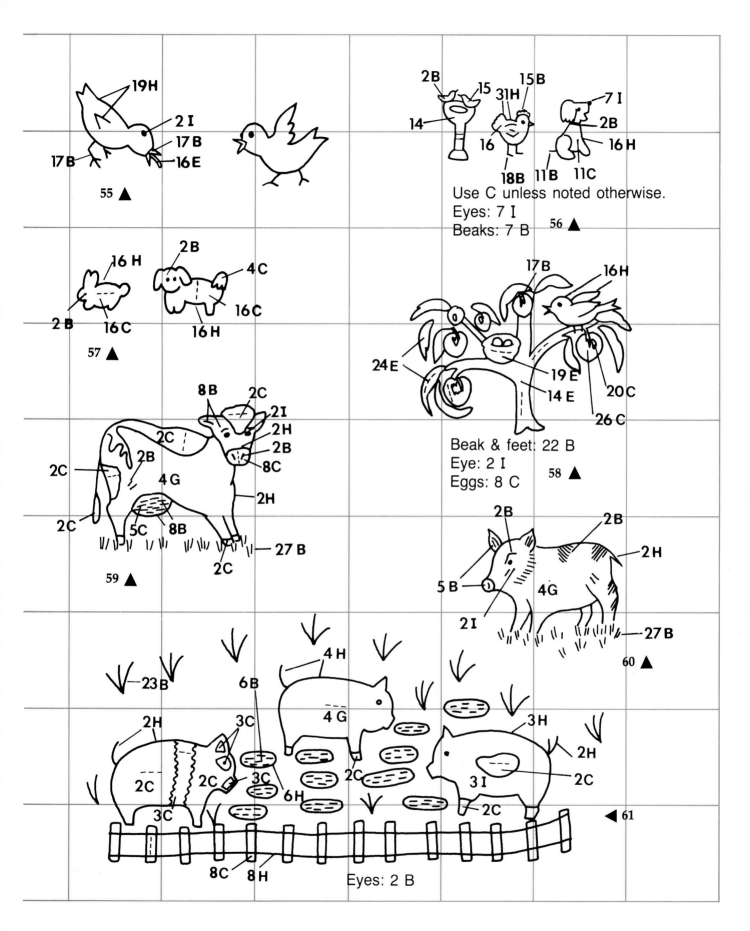

19H

2 I

17 B

17 B 16 E

55 ▲

2B

15

15B

31H

7 I

14

2B

16

16 H

18B 11B 11C

Use C unless noted otherwise.
Eyes: 7 I
Beaks: 7 B    56 ▲

16 H

2B

4C

2 B

16C

16C

16 H

57 ▲

17B

16H

24E

19 E

14 E

20C

26 C

Beak & feet: 22 B
Eye: 2 I
Eggs: 8 C    58 ▲

8 B

2C

2I

2H

2C

2B

2C

8C

2B

2H

2C

4 G

2C

5C

8B

27 B

59 ▲

2C

2B

2B

2H

5 B

4G

2H

2 I

27 B

60 ▲

4 H

23 B

6 B

2H

4 G

3 H

3C

2H

2C

3C

2C

2C

3I

2C

3C

6H

2C

◄ 61

8C    8 H

Eyes: 2 B

63

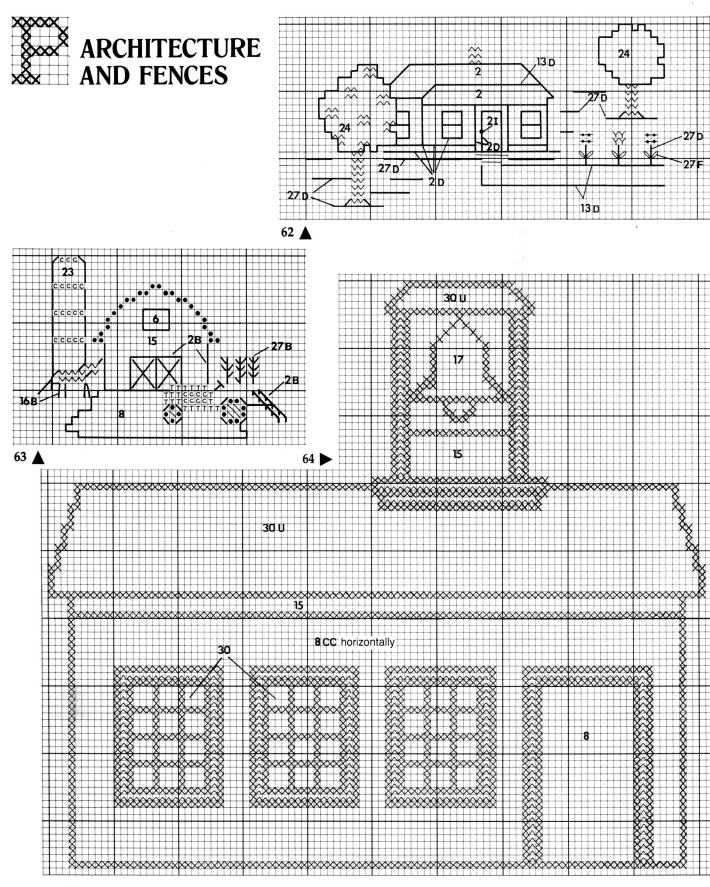

# ARCHITECTURE AND FENCES

62 ▲

63 ▲

64 ▶

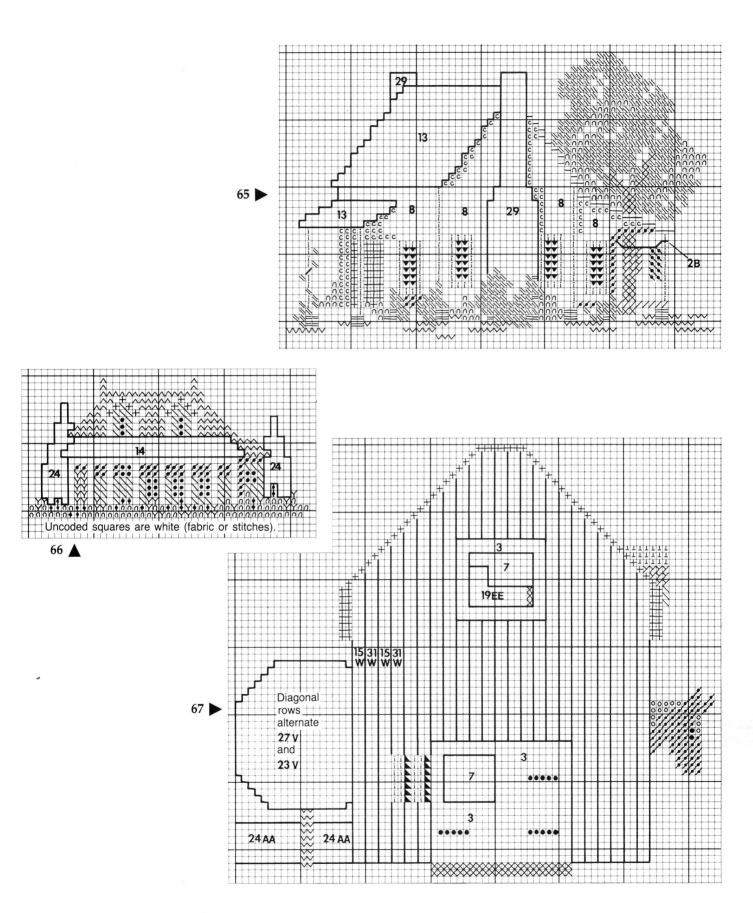

**65** ▶

29

13

13  8  8  29  8  8

2B

**66** ▲

24

14

24

Uncoded squares are white (fabric or stitches).

**67** ▶

3

7

19EE

15 31 15 31
W W W W

Diagonal
rows
alternate
**27 V**
and
**23 V**

3

7

3

24 AA    24 AA

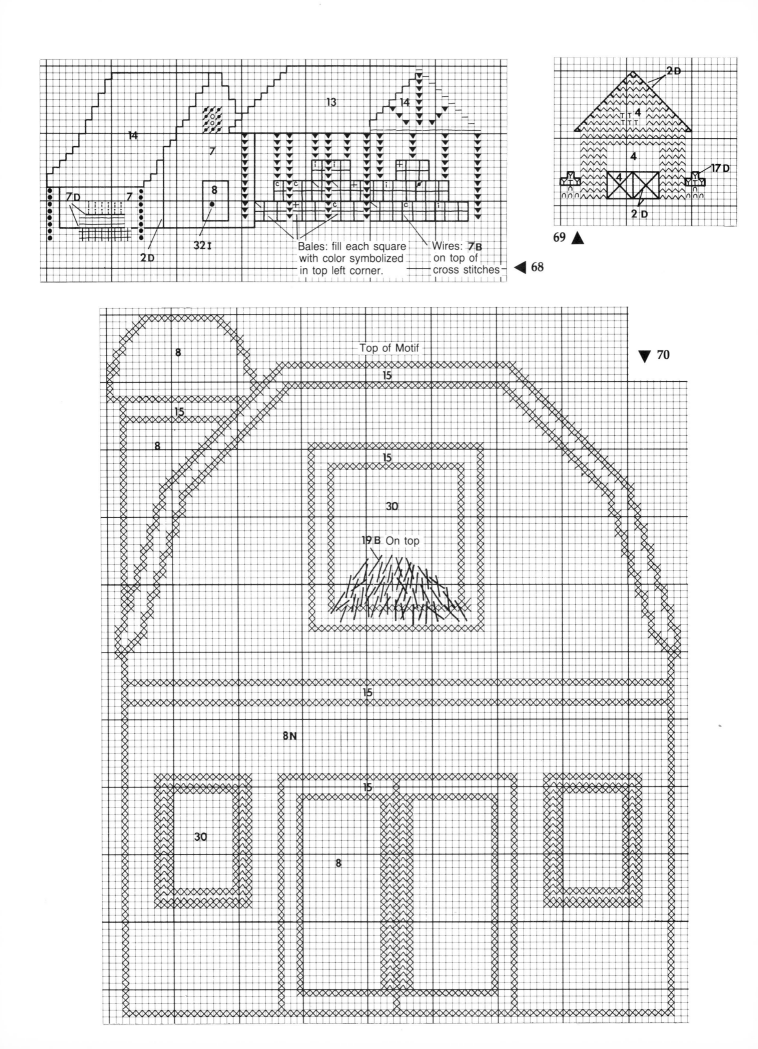

13

14

14

7

7D 7

8

2D

32 I

Bales: fill each square
with color symbolized
in top left corner.

Wires: 7B
on top of
cross stitches

◀ 68

2 D

4

4

17 D

4

2 D

69 ▲

8

Top of Motif

15

15

8

15

30

19 B On top

15

8 N

30

8

15

▼ 70

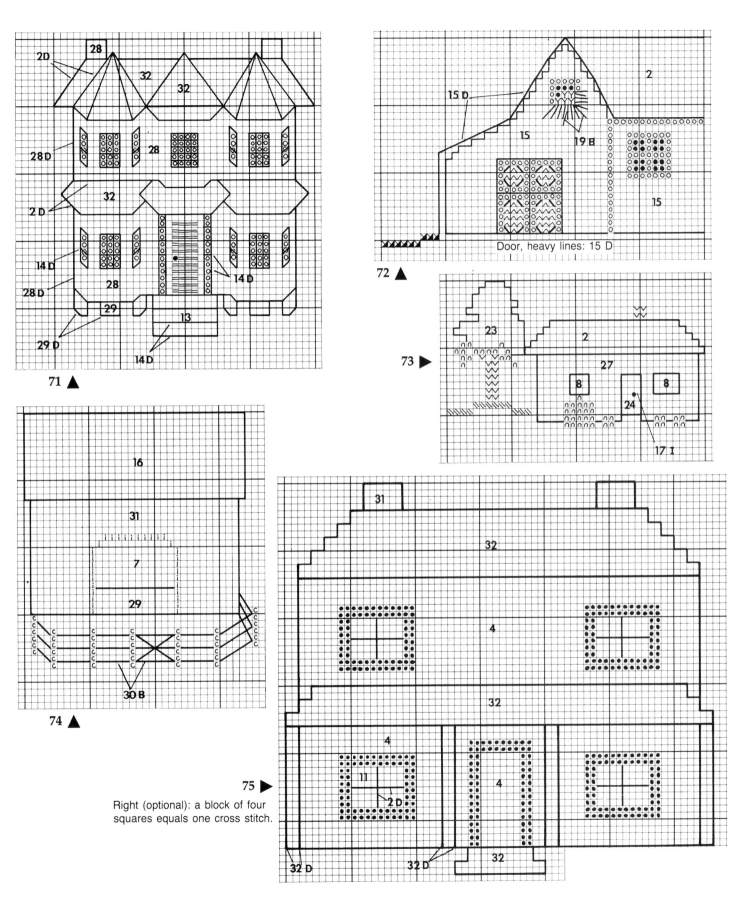

2D

28

32

32

28D

28

2D

32

14D

28D

28

14D

29

13

29D

14D

71 ▲

15 D

2

15

19 B

15

Door, heavy lines: 15 D

72 ▲

73 ▶

23

2

27

8

8

24

17 I

16

31

7

29

c c c c c c c c c c c c c c c c c c c c c c c c c c c c c c c c c c c c c c c c c c

30 B

74 ▲

31

32

4

32

4

11

2 D

4

32 D

32 D

32

75 ▶

Right (optional): a block of four
squares equals one cross stitch.

67

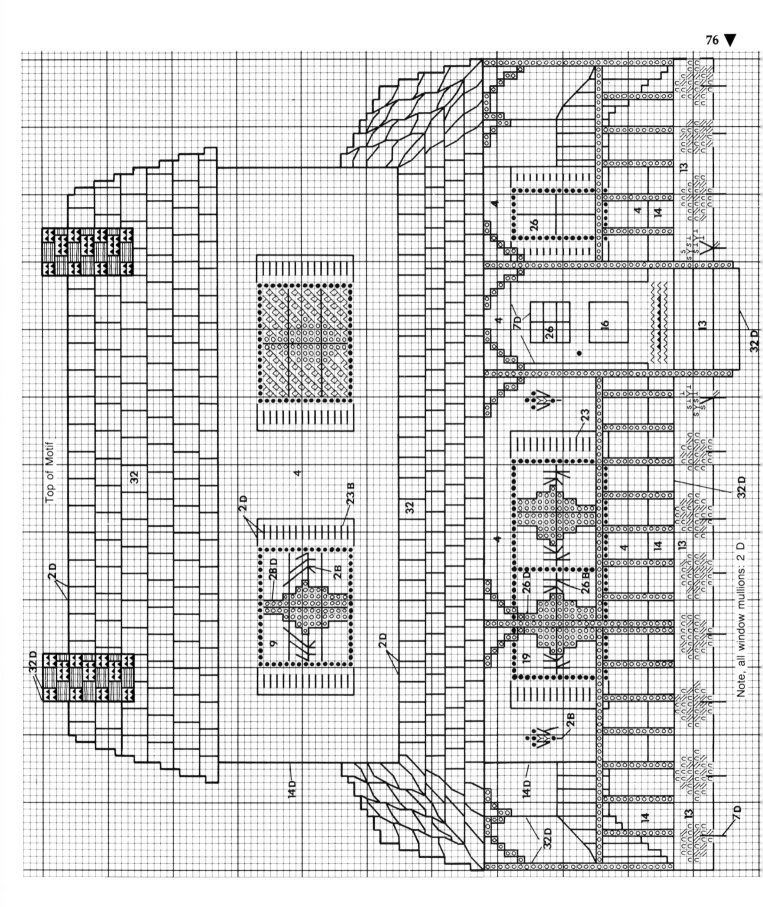

Top of Motif

32

2 D

32 D

4

2 D

2 D

2 D

2 B D

2 B

23 B

9

14 D

32

4

26

7 D

26

16

13

4

14

13

32 D

4

14 D

4

23

19

26 D

26 B

4

14

13

32 D

14

13

7 D

Note, all window mullions: 2 D

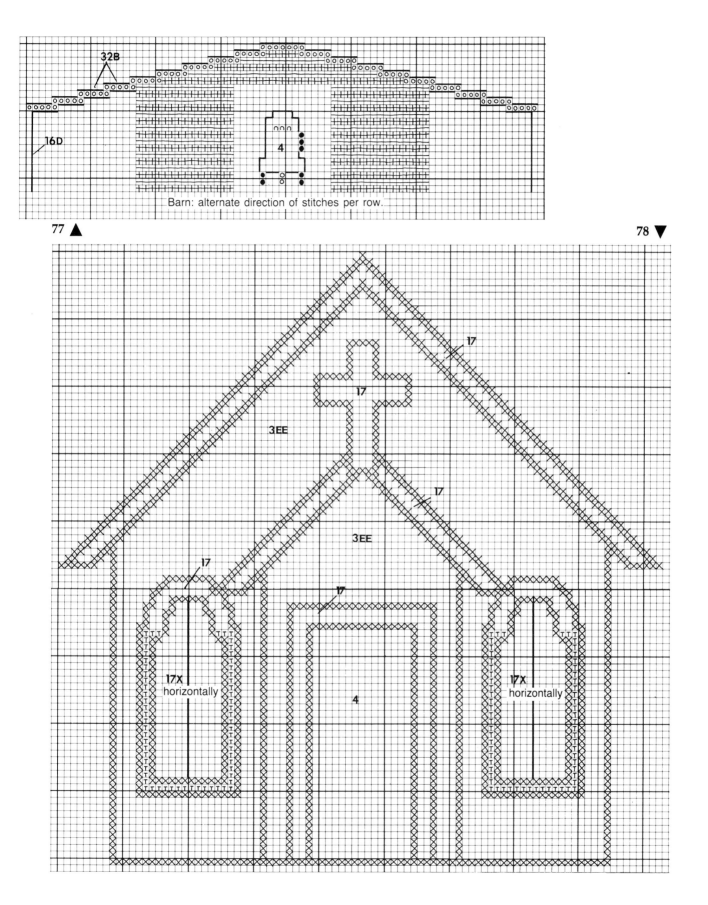

Barn: alternate direction of stitches per row.

32B

16D

4

77 ▲

78 ▼

17

17

3EE

17

3EE

17

17

17X
horizontally

4

17X
horizontally

69

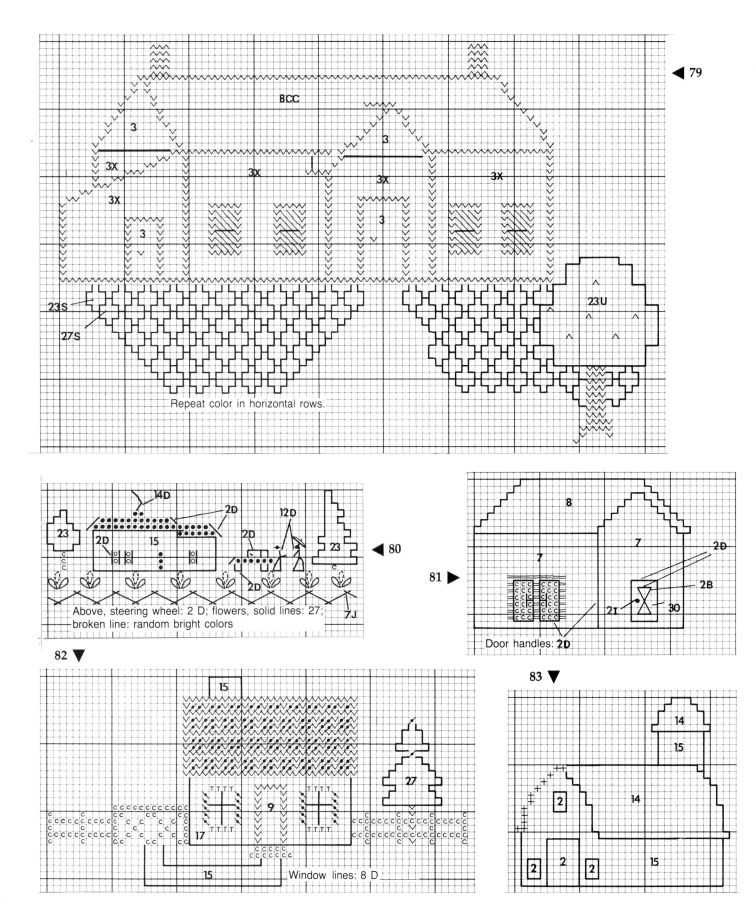

◀ 79

BCC

3

3          3

3X        3X        3X          3X

3X

3          3

23S

27S

23U

Repeat color in horizontal rows.

14D
2D
12D
23          2D
2D      15                    2D    23
◀ 80
2D
7J

Above, steering wheel: 2 D; flowers, solid lines: 27;
broken line: random bright colors

82 ▼

8
7        7
2D
81 ▶        7
2B
21        30

Door handles: 2D

83 ▼

15
27
c c c c c c c c c c        9
c c c c c c c c c c    c c        c c c c c c c c c c c
c c c c c c c c c c  c c  c c  c c c c c c c c c c c c c c c
c c c c c c c c c c  c c    c c    c c c c c c c c c c c c c c
c c        c c        c c c c c c c c
17          c c c c c
                  c c c c c
15                  c c c c c
Window lines: 8 D

14
15
2          14
2      2      2      15

70

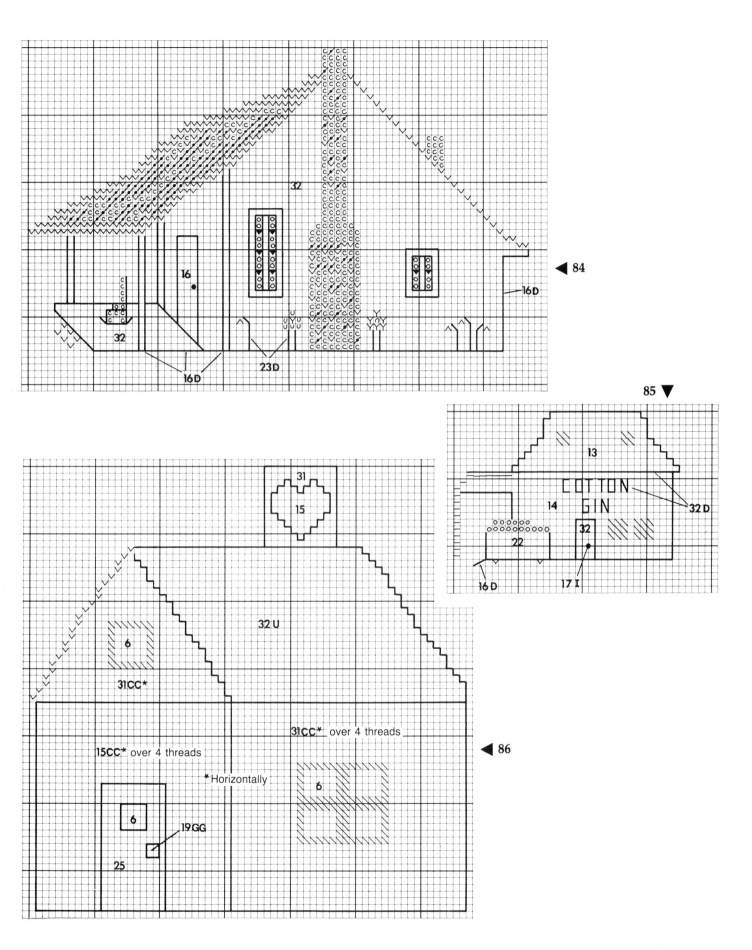

◄ 84

16 D

32

16 D

23 D

85 ▼

13

COTTON
GIN

14

32 D

22

32

16 D

17 I

31

15

32 U

6

31CC*

31CC* over 4 threads

15CC* over 4 threads

◄ 86

*Horizontally

6

6

19 GG

25

71

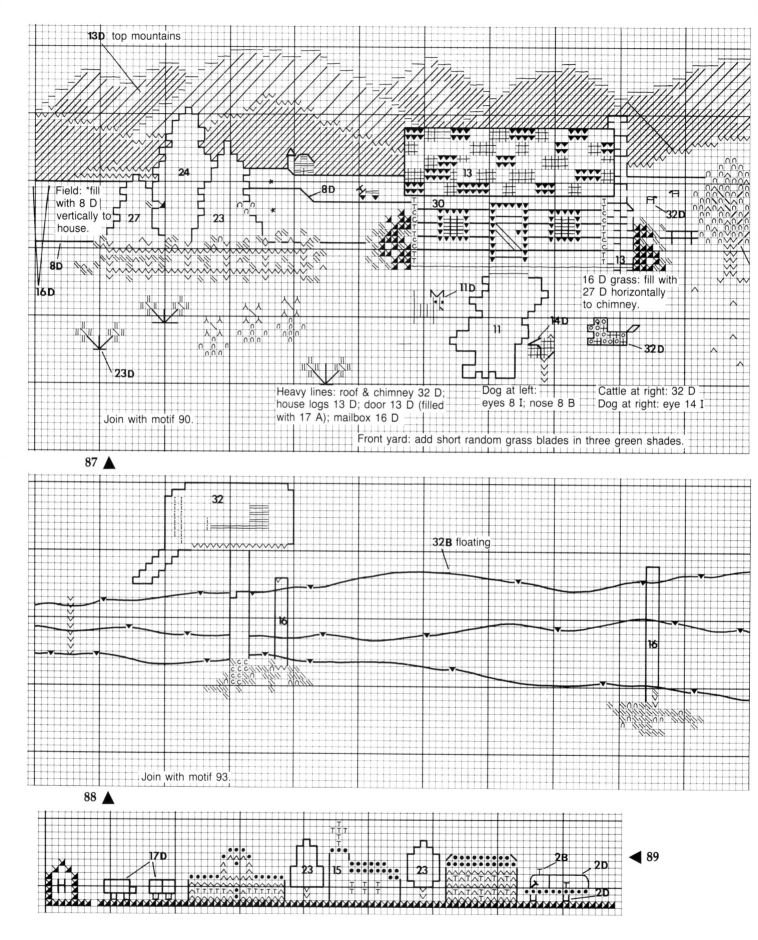

**13 D** top mountains

24

Field: *fill with 8 D vertically to house.

27    23

8 D

**8 D**

**16 D**

23 D

13

30

**8 D**

11 D

16 D grass: fill with 27 D horizontally to chimney.

11    14 D

13

32 D

32 D

Heavy lines: roof & chimney 32 D; house logs 13 D; door 13 D (filled with 17 A); mailbox 16 D

Dog at left: eyes 8 I; nose 8 B

Cattle at right: 32 D Dog at right: eye 14 I

Join with motif 90.

Front yard: add short random grass blades in three green shades.

**87** ▲

32

**32 B** floating

16

16

Join with motif 93.

**88** ▲

17 D

23    15    23

2 B

2 D

◀ **89**

2 D

72

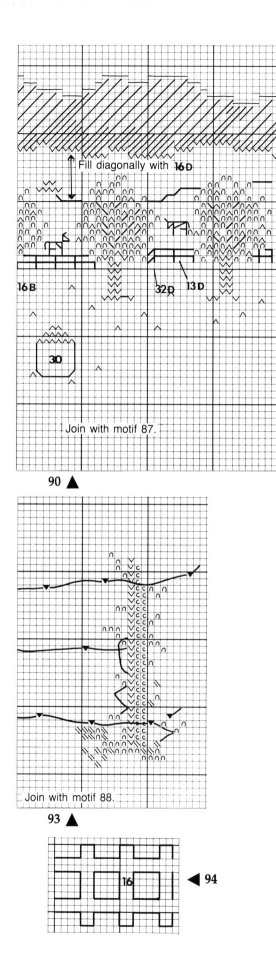

Fill diagonally with 16 D

16 B   32 D   13 D

30

Join with motif 87.

90 ▲

Join with motif 88.

93 ▲

16   ◀ 94

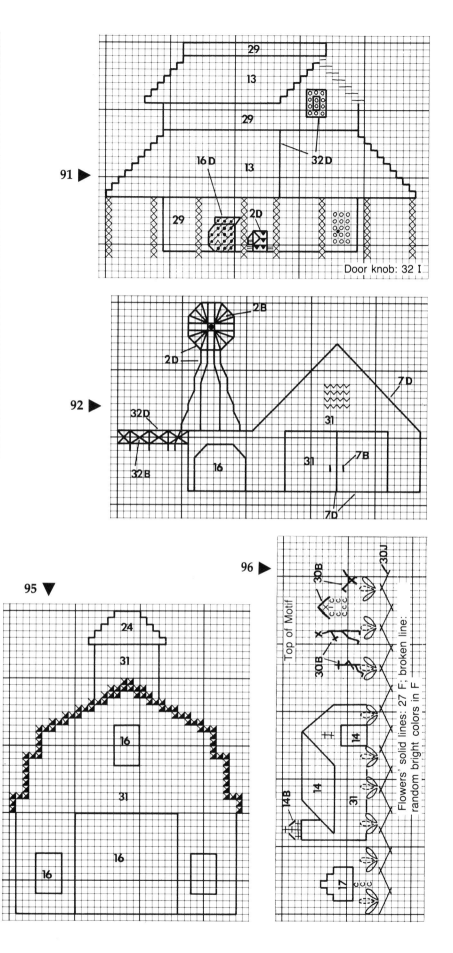

91 ▶

29

13

29

16 D   13   32 D

29   2 D

Door knob: 32 I

92 ▶

2 B

2 D

7 D

32 D   31

32 B   16   31   7 B

7 D

95 ▼

24

31

16

31

16   16

96 ▶

Top of Motif

30 B   30 J

30 B

14

14 B   14   31

17

Flowers' solid lines: 27 F; broken line:
random bright colors in F

73

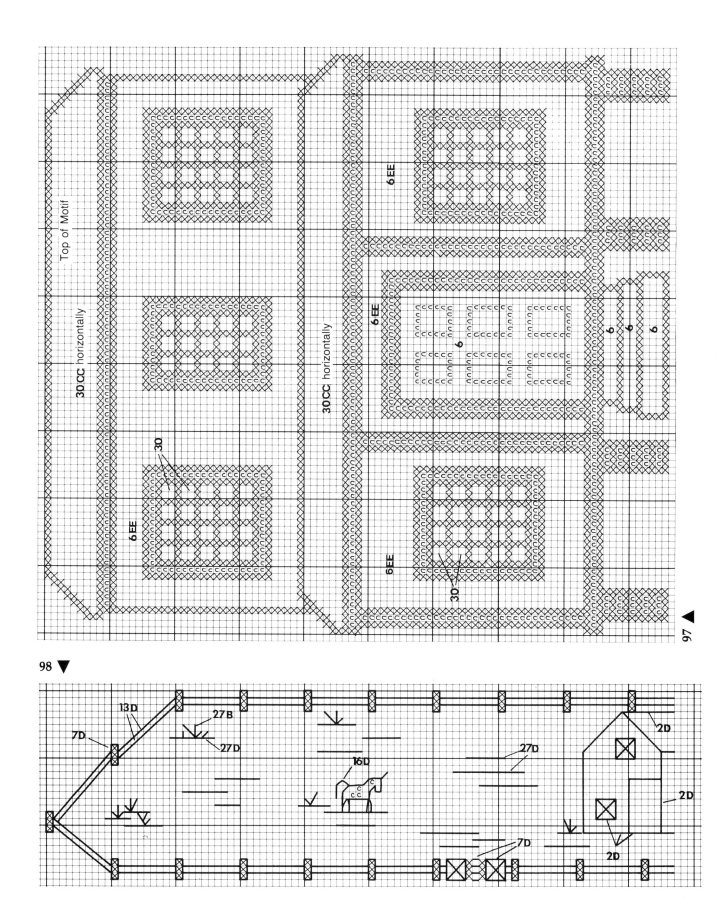

Top of Motif

30CC horizontally

30CC horizontally

6EE

6EE

6EE

6EE

6EE

30

30

6

6

6

6

97 ▲

98 ▼

13D

7D

27B

27D

16D

27D

2D

2D

7D

2D

74

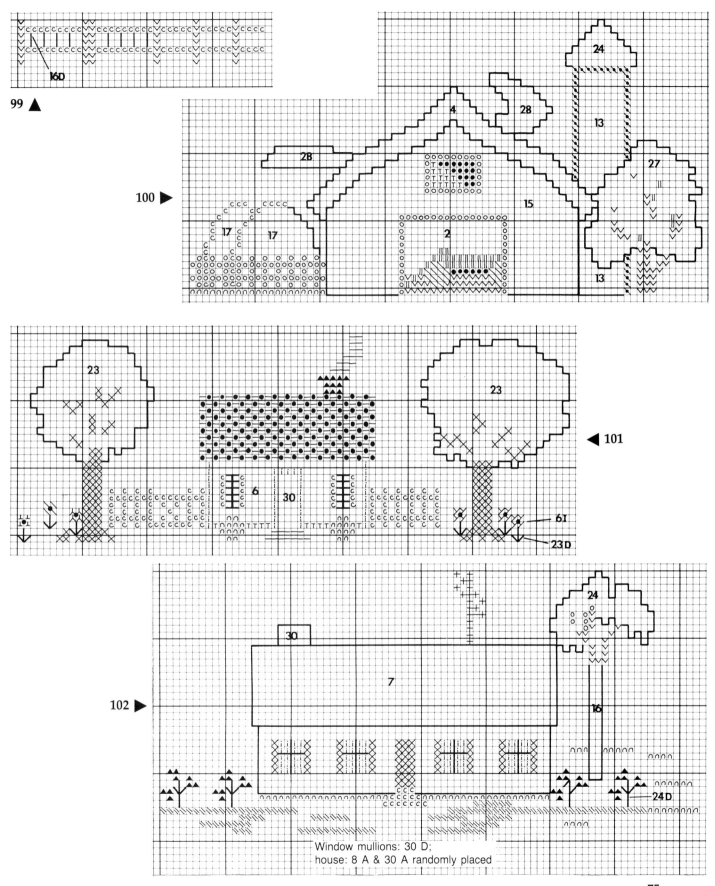

Window mullions: 30 D;
house: 8 A & 30 A randomly placed

75

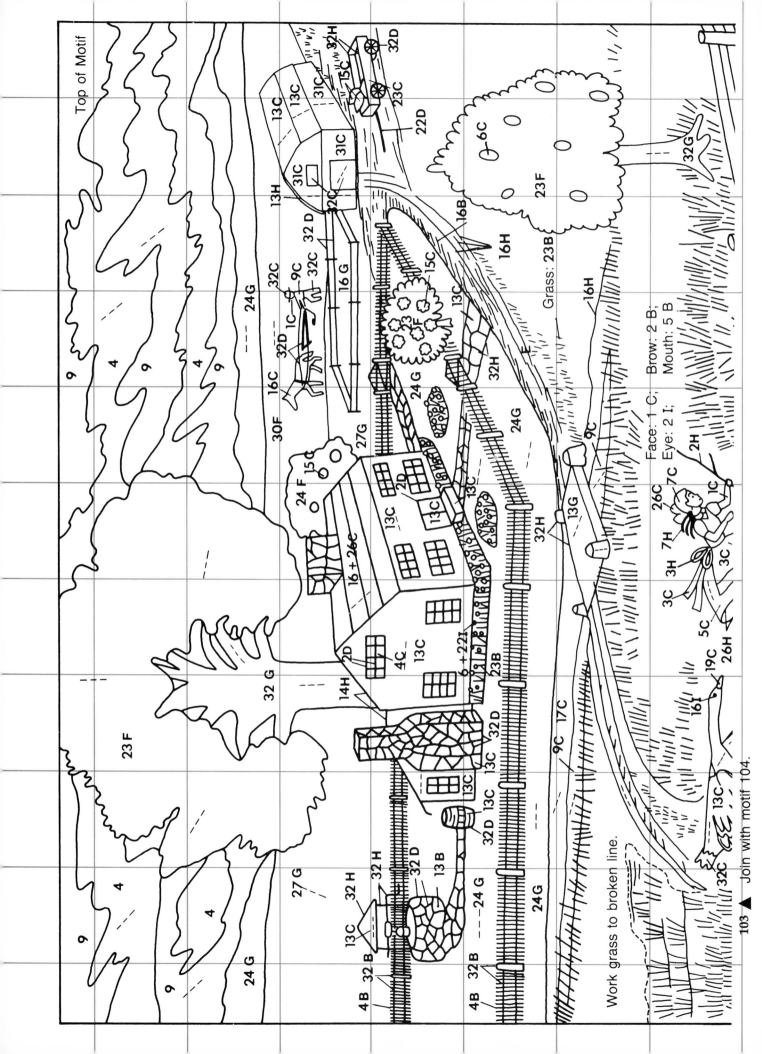

Top of Motif

103 ▲ Join with motif 104.

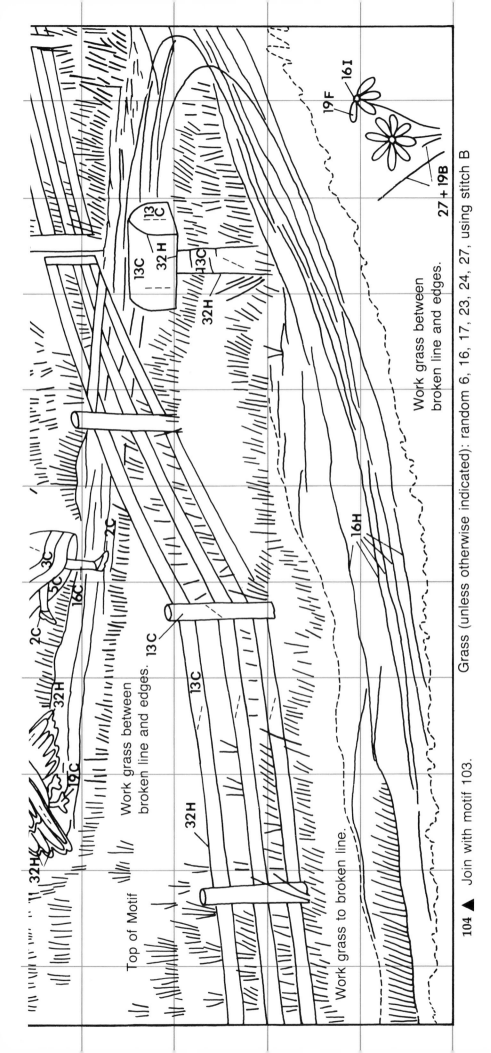

Top of Motif

Work grass between
broken line and edges. 13C

Work grass between
broken line and edges.

Work grass to broken line.

Work grass between
broken line and edges.

27 + 19B

104 ▲  Join with motif 103.

Grass (unless otherwise indicated): random 6, 16, 17, 23, 24, 27, using stitch B

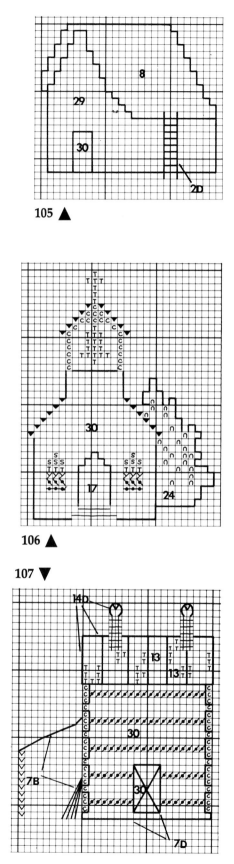

105 ▲

106 ▲

107 ▼

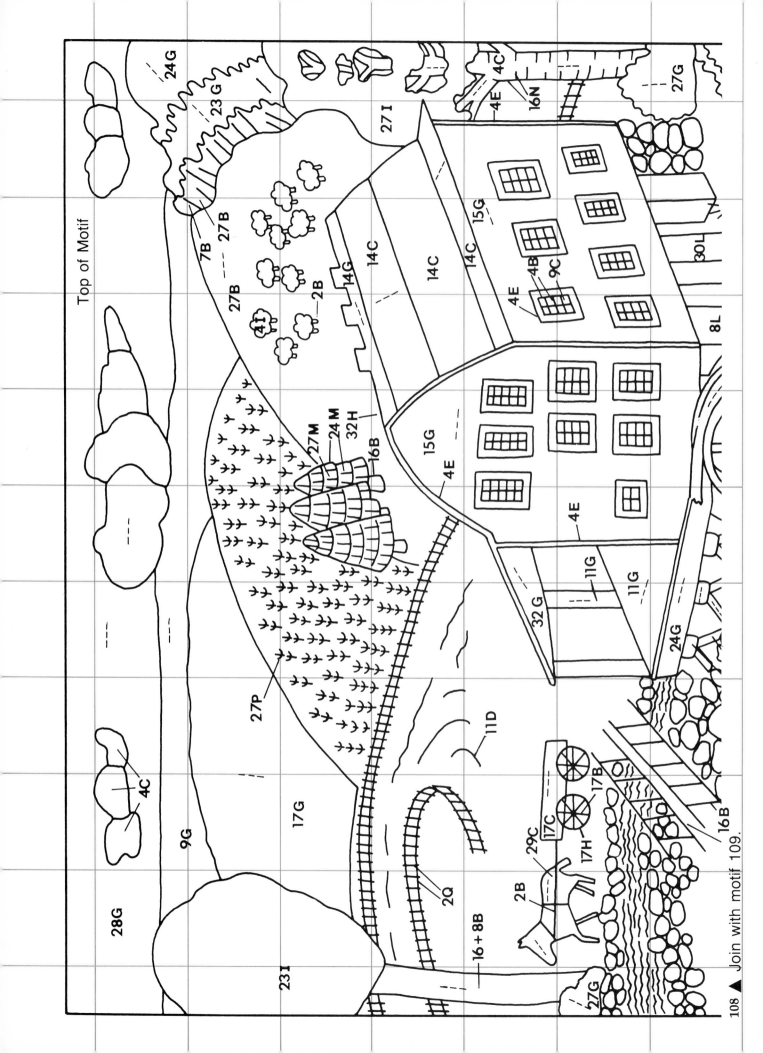

Top of Motif

28G

24G

23G

9G

4C

17G

23I

16 + 8B

2Q

11D

27P

27M
24M
32H
16B

15G

4E

7B
27B

27B
2B

4I

23 G

24 G

27 B

14G

14C

14C

14C

14C

15G

4E
4B
9C

4E

4E

4E

27 I

15G

4E

4C
4C

16N

27G

32 G

11G

11G

24G

2B
29C

17C
17H

17B

30L

8L

27G

16B

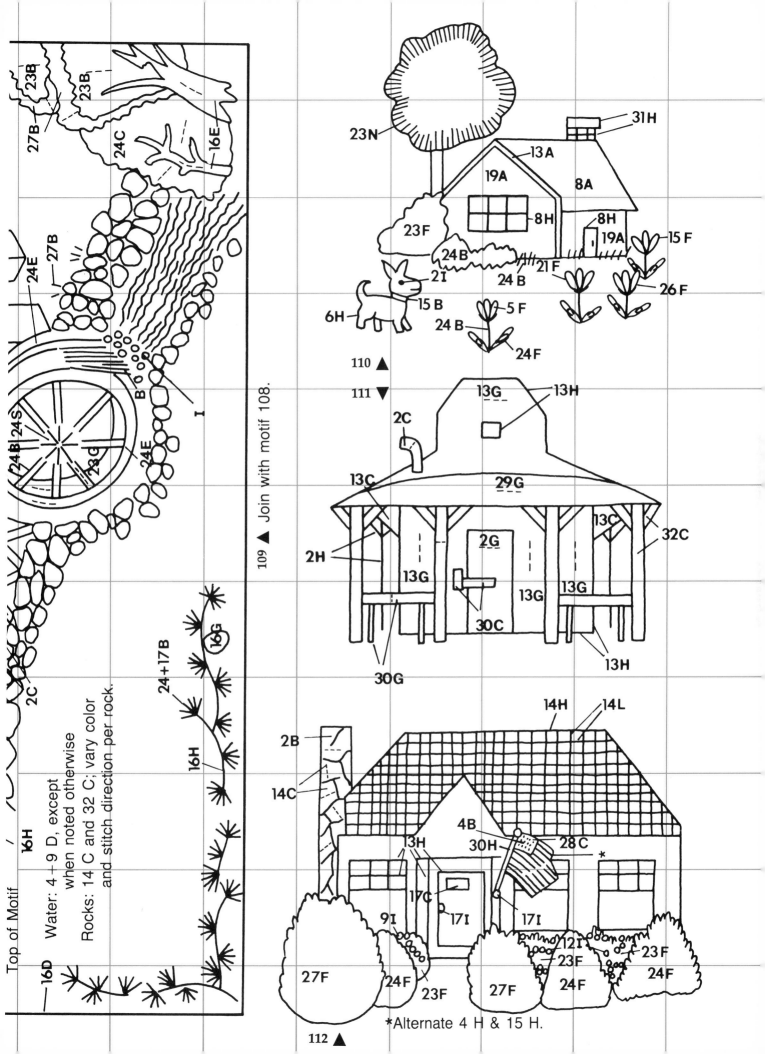

Top of Motif

23B
23B
27B
24C
16E

24E
27B

24B 24S
23G
24E
B
I
2C

16H

16D
**16H**

Water: 4 + 9 D, except
when noted otherwise
Rocks: 14 C and 32 C; vary color
and stitch direction per rock.

24+17B
16G
16H

109 ▲ Join with motif 108.

23N
31H
13A
19A
8A
23F
8H
8H
19A
15 F
24 B
21 F
24 B
26 F
21
15 B
5 F
6H
24 B
24 F

110 ▲

111 ▼

13G
13H
2C
13C
29G
13C
32C
2H
2G
13G
13G
13G
30C
30G
13H

14H
14L
2B
14C
4B
3H
30H
28 C
17C
*
9 I
17 I
17 I
12 I
27F
23 F
23F
27F
24 F
24 F
23 F
23 F
24F

*Alternate 4 H & 15 H.

112 ▲

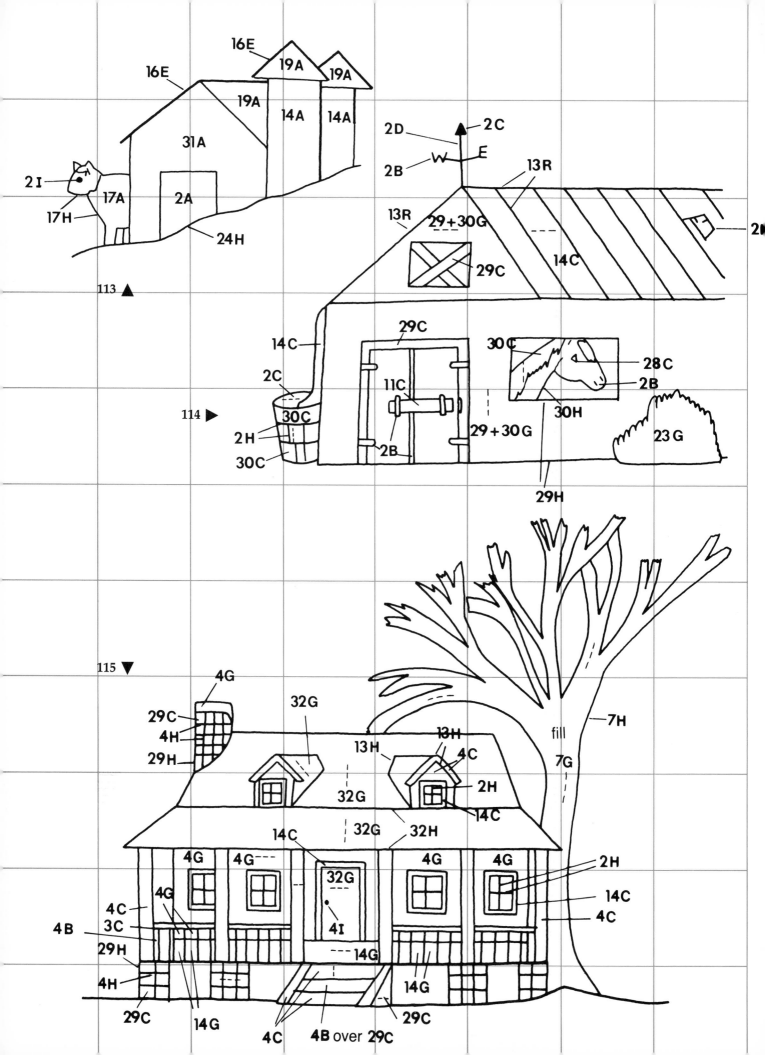

 **BORDERS**

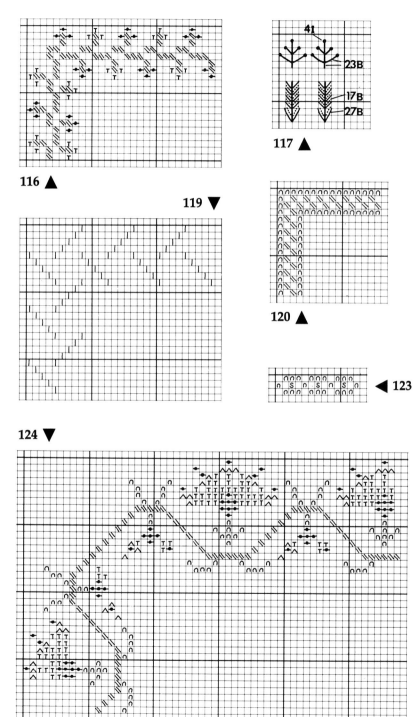

116 ▲

117 ▲

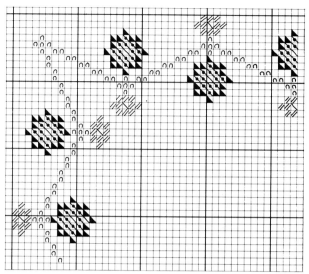

118 ▲

119 ▼

120 ▲

121 ▲

◄ 123

122 ▶

124 ▼

125 ▼

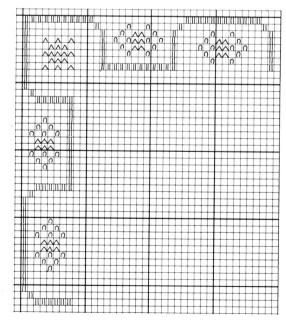

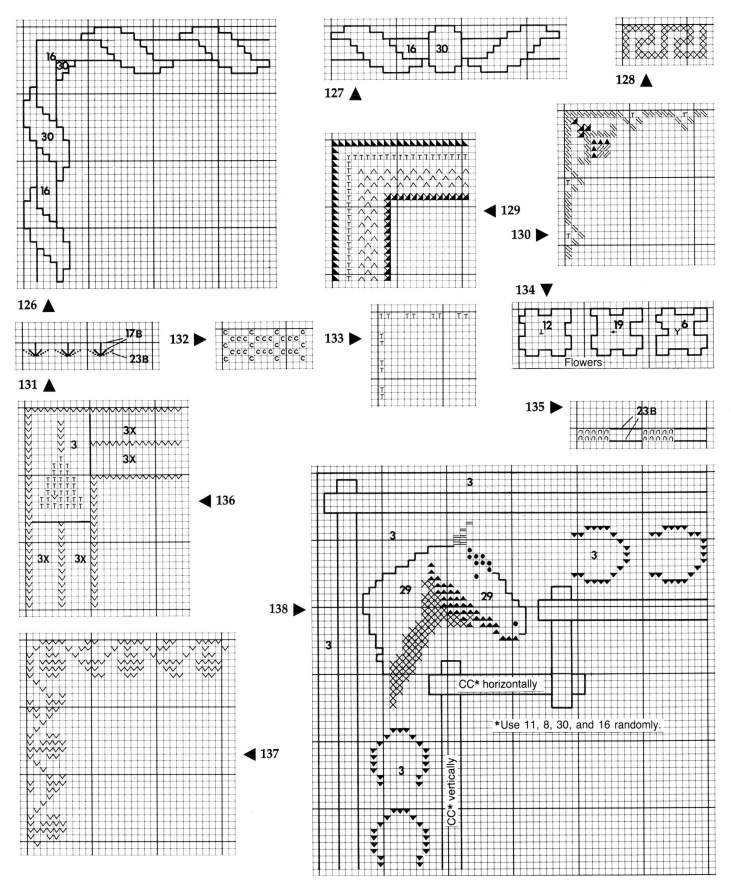

126 ▲

127 ▲

128 ▲

◀ 129

130 ▶

131 ▲

132 ▶

133 ▶

134 ▼

135 ▶

◀ 136

◀ 137

138 ▶

Flowers

CC* horizontally

*Use 11, 8, 30, and 16 randomly.

CC* vertically

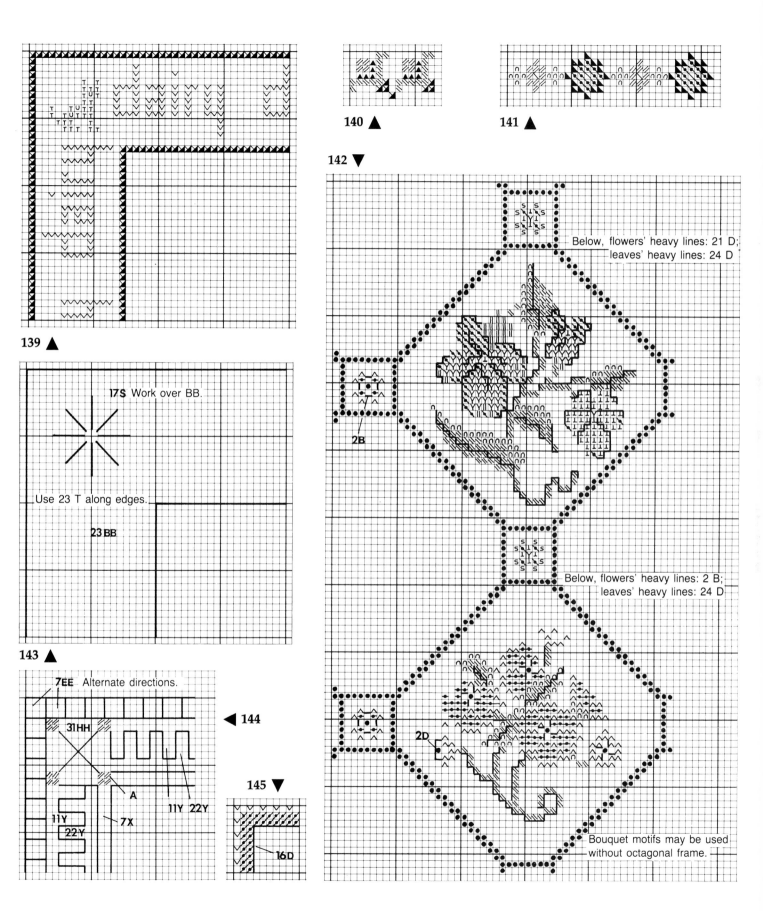

**139** ▲

**140** ▲

**141** ▲

**142** ▼

**143** ▲

17 S Work over BB.

Use 23 T along edges.

23 BB

7 EE Alternate directions.

31 HH

A

11 Y

22 Y

11 Y 22 Y

7 X

◄ **144**

**145** ▼

16 D

Below, flowers' heavy lines: 21 D;
leaves' heavy lines: 24 D

2 B

Below, flowers' heavy lines: 2 B;
leaves' heavy lines: 24 D

2 D

Bouquet motifs may be used
without octagonal frame.

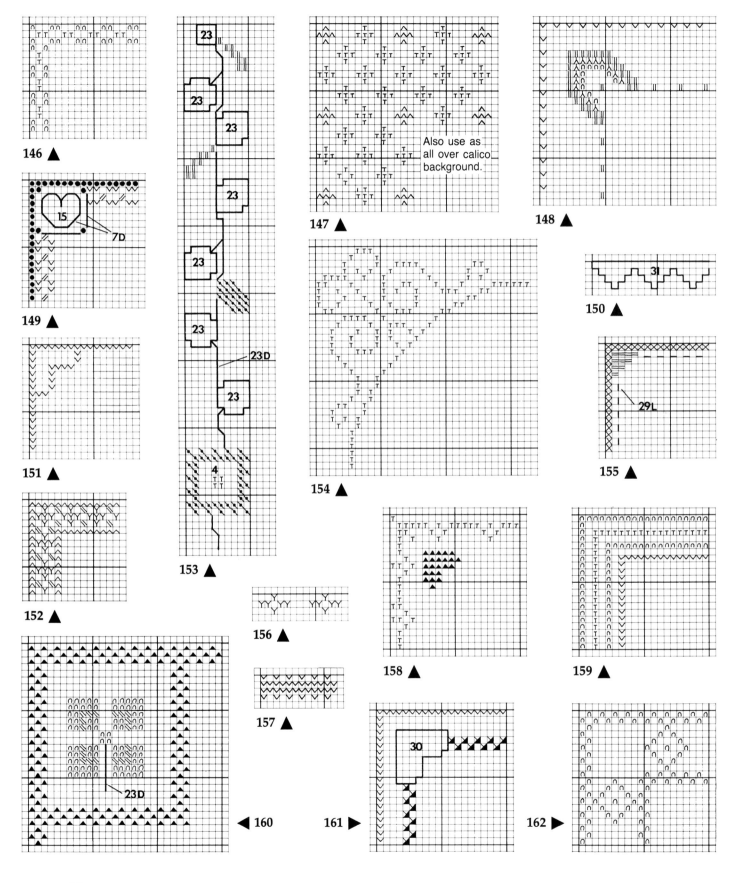

**146** ▲

**149** ▲

**151** ▲

**152** ▲

**153** ▲

**23D**

**23**

**23**

**23**

**23**

**23**

**23**

**23D**

**4**

**15**

**7D**

**147** ▲

Also use as all over calico background.

**148** ▲

**150** ▲

**31**

**154** ▲

**155** ▲

**29L**

**156** ▲

**157** ▲

**158** ▲

**159** ▲

**160** ◀

**23D**

**161** ▶

**30**

**162** ▶

84

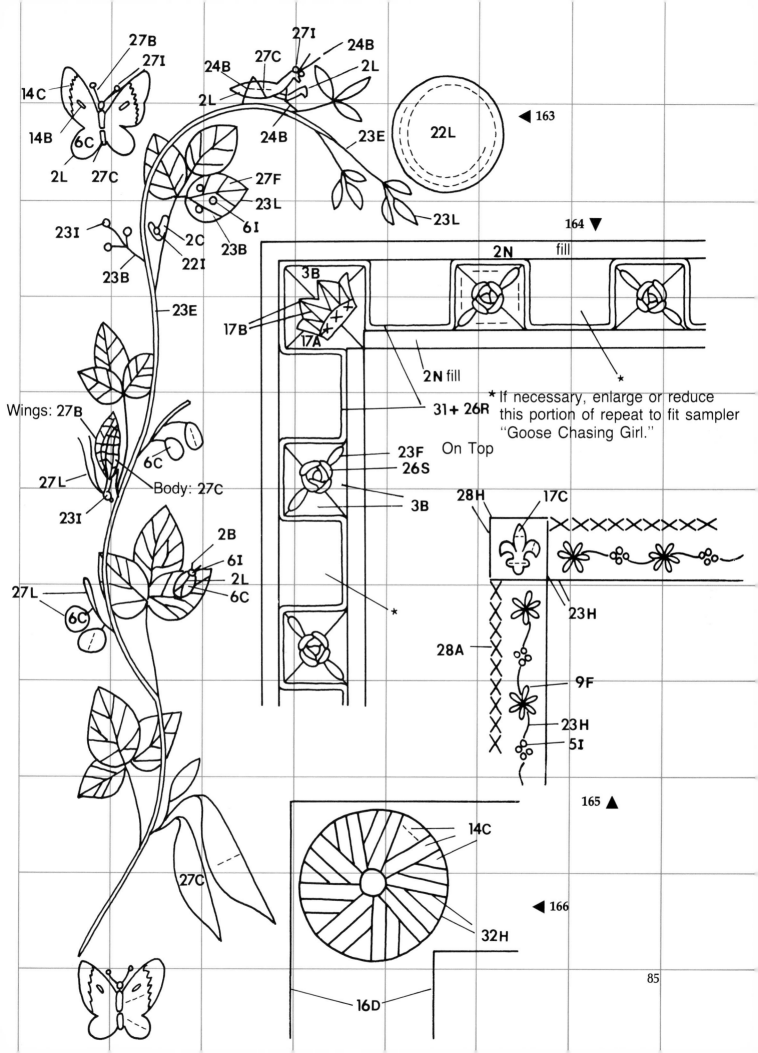

27B
27I
14C
14B
6C
2L  27C

24B
27C
27I
24B
2L
2L
24B
23E

22L
◀ 163

164 ▼

27F
23L
6I
23B
2C
22I
23I
23B
23B

23E

3B
17B
17A
2N  fill
2N fill
31+ 26R

* If necessary, enlarge or reduce
this portion of repeat to fit sampler
"Goose Chasing Girl."

On Top

23F
26S
3B

28H    17C
28A

XXXXXXXXXX

23H

9F
23H
5I

165 ▲

Wings: 27B
6C
27L
Body: 27C
23I

2B
6I
2L
6C
27L
6C

*

14C

27C

◀ 166

32H

16D

85

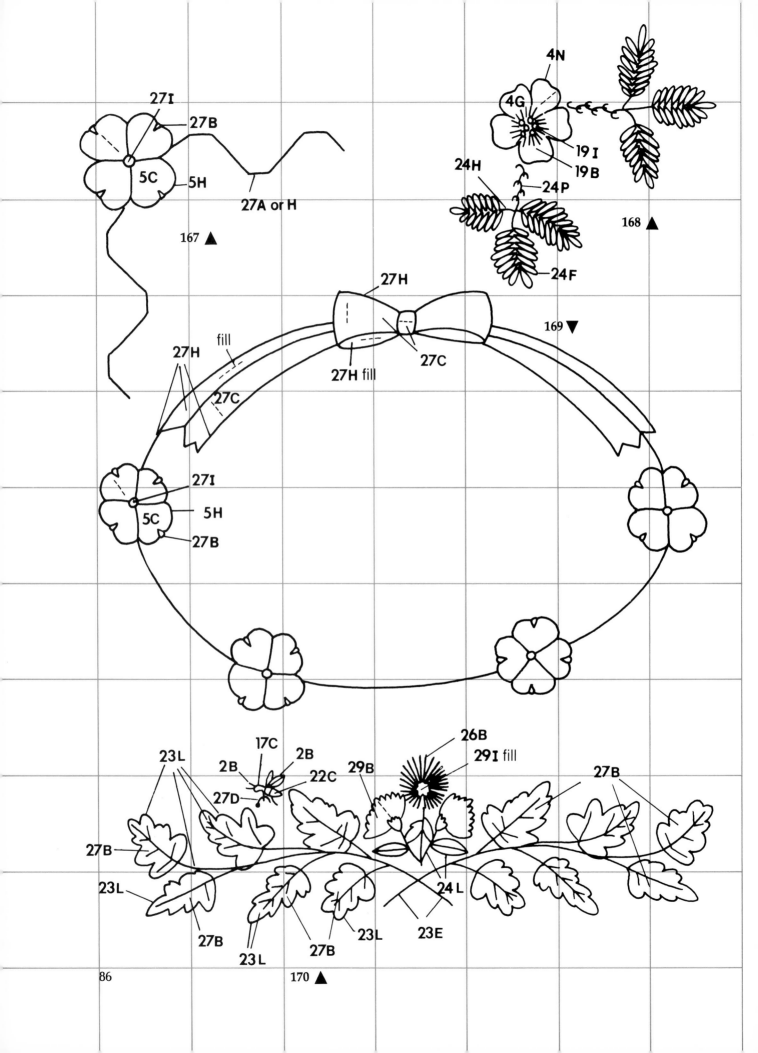

27I

27B

5C

5H

27A or H

167 ▲

4N

4G

19 I

19 B

24H

24P

24F

168 ▲

27H

169 ▼

27H fill

27C

27H

fill

27C

27I

5C

5H

27B

17C

2B

2B

22C

26B

29I fill

27B

23L

27D

29B

27B

27B

23L

24 L

23L

23E

23 L

27B

23 L

27B

86

170 ▲

# CROPS, FRUITS, AND VEGETABLES

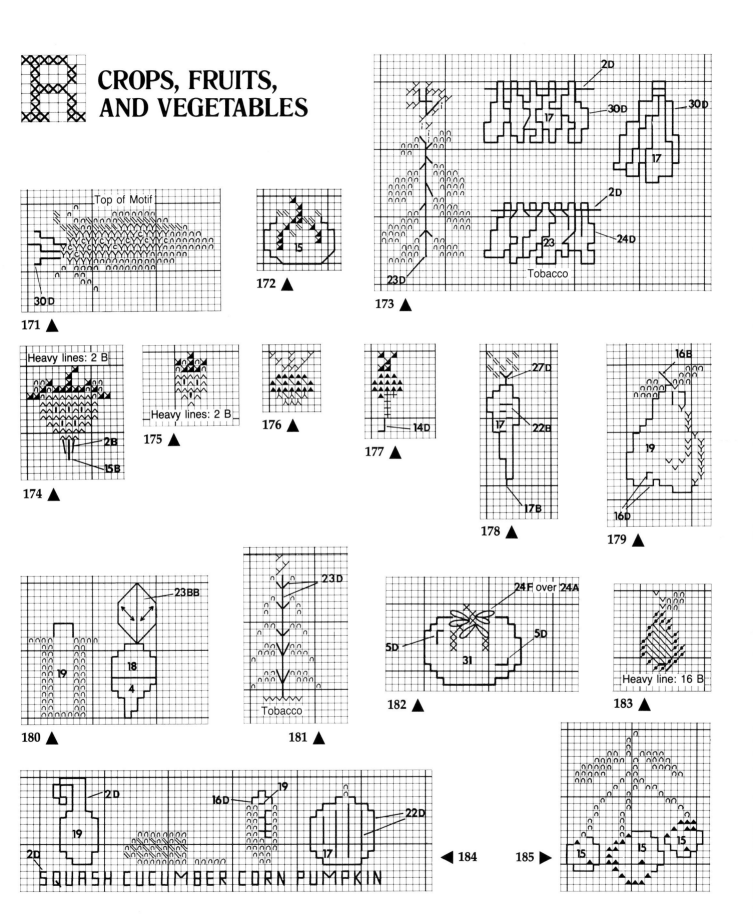

171 ▲

172 ▲

173 ▲  Tobacco

174 ▲  Heavy lines: 2 B  2B  15B

175 ▲  Heavy lines: 2 B

176 ▲

177 ▲  14D

178 ▲  27D  22B  17B

179 ▲  16B  16D

180 ▲  23BB

181 ▲  23D  Tobacco

182 ▲  24F over 24A  5D

183 ▲  Heavy line: 16 B

SQUASH  CUCUMBER  CORN  PUMPKIN

◀ 184

185 ▶

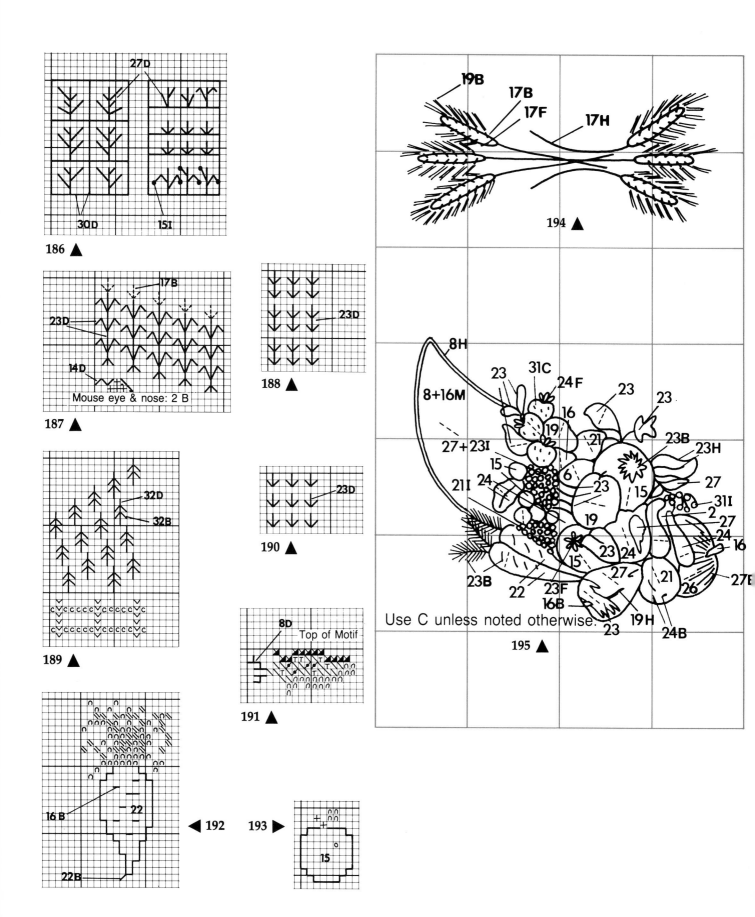

27D

30D    15I

186 ▲

17B

23D

14D

Mouse eye & nose: 2 B

187 ▲

23D

188 ▲

32D

32B

CCCCCCCCCC
CCCCCCCCCCCC

189 ▲

23D

190 ▲

8D    Top of Motif

191 ▲

16 B    22

22B

◀ 192    193 ▶

15

19B    17B

17F    17H

194 ▲

8H

8+16M

27+23I

21I    24    15    6    23    15    27    31I    2    27    24    16

23    31C    24F    23    23    16    21    23B    23H    19

15    19    23    24    23F    16B    19H    24B    21    27    26    27E

23B    22    23    Use C unless noted otherwise.

195 ▲

88

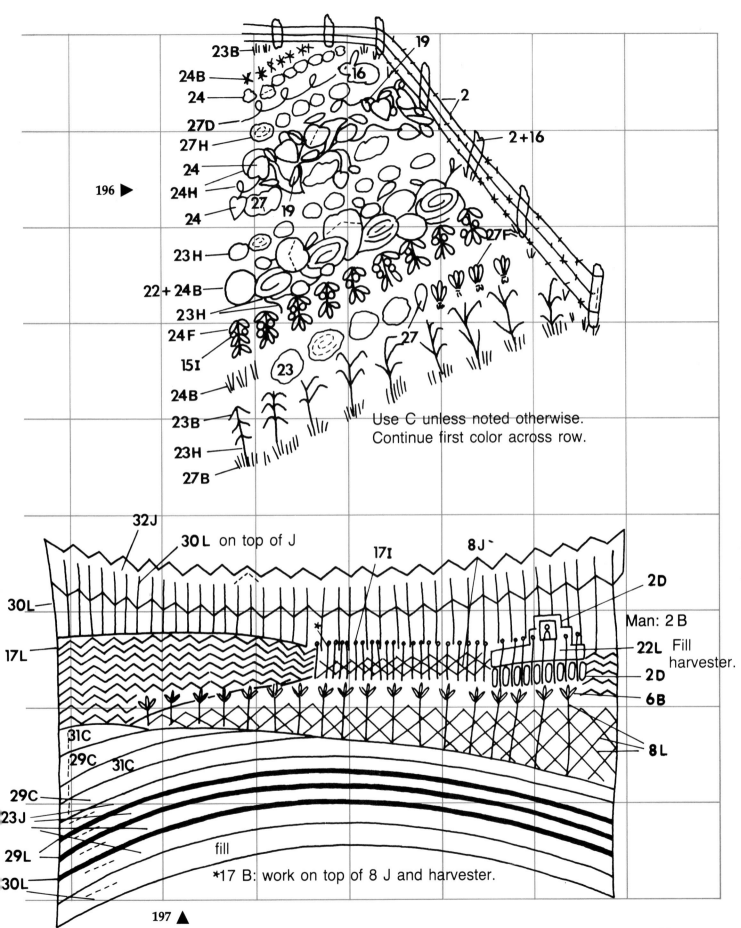

23B

24B

24

27D

27H

24

24H

196 ▶

24

23H

22+24B

23H

24F

15I

24B

23B

23H

27B

19

2

2+16

27F

27

16

27

19

23

Use C unless noted otherwise.
Continue first color across row.

32J

30L on top of J

17I

8J

2D

30L

Man: 2B

17L

22L Fill
harvester.

2D

6B

31C

8L

29C

31C

29C

23J

29L

fill

30L

*17 B: work on top of 8 J and harvester.

197 ▲

# FLOWERS

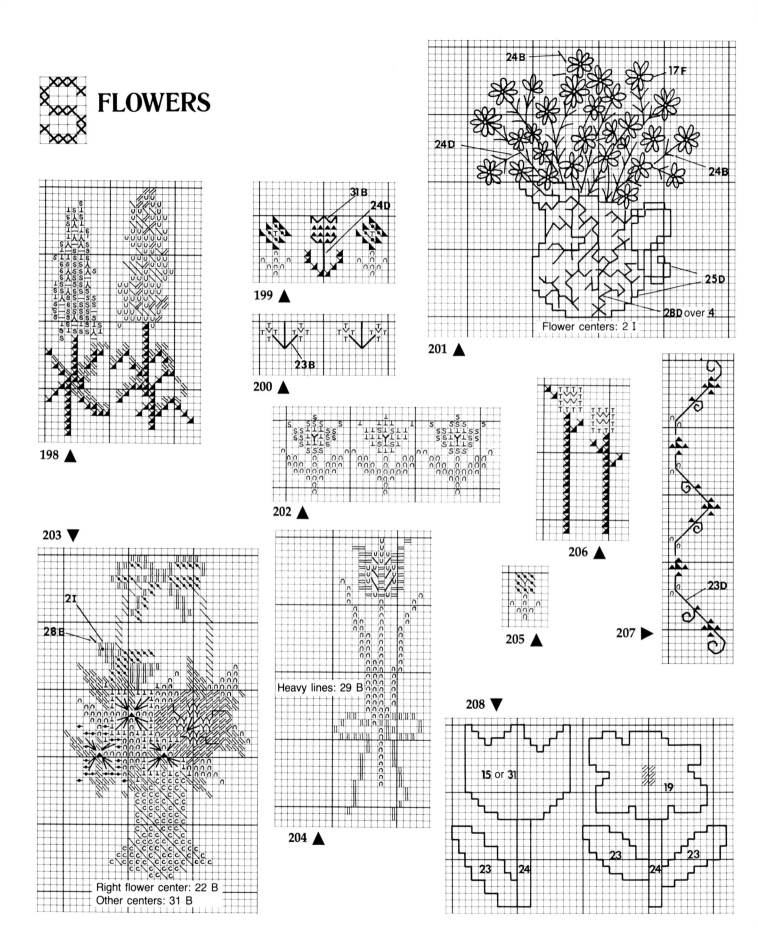

**198** ▲

**199** ▲

**200** ▲
23B

**201** ▲
24B
17F
24D
24B
25D
28D over 4
Flower centers: 2 I

**202** ▲

**203** ▼
2I
28B
Right flower center: 22 B
Other centers: 31 B

**204** ▲
Heavy lines: 29 B

**205** ▲

**206** ▲

**207** ▶
23D

**208** ▼
15 or 31
19
23
23
23
24

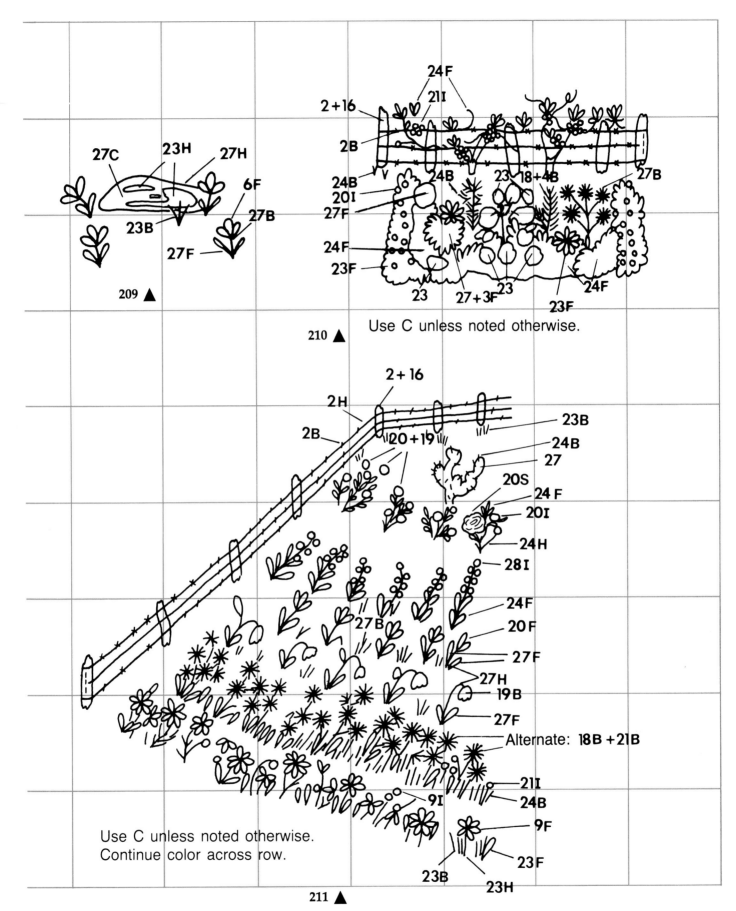

27C  23H  27H

6F

23B  27B

27F

209 ▲

24F

21I

2+16

2B

24B
20I
27F

24B  23  18+4B  27B

24F
23F

23  27+3F  23  24F

23F

Use C unless noted otherwise.

210 ▲

2+16

2H

2B

20+19

23B

24B

27

20S

24F

20I

24H

28I

27B

24F

20F

27F

27H

19B

27F

Alternate: 18B+21B

21I

24B

9I

9F

9F

23F

Use C unless noted otherwise.
Continue color across row.

23B

23H

211 ▲

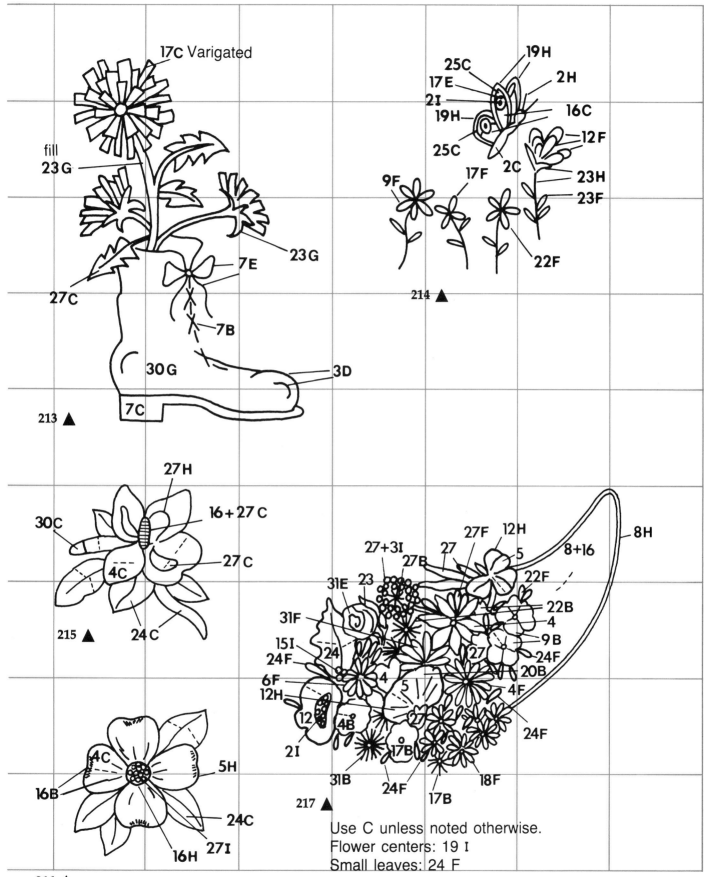

17C Varigated

fill
23G

27C

7E

7B

30G

3D

7C

213 ▲

25C

19H

17E

2H

2I

19H

16C

25C

2C

12F

9F

17F

23H

23F

22F

214 ▲

27H

16 + 27 C

30C

27C

4C

24C

215 ▲

4C

5H

16B

24C

16H    27I

216 ▲

27F    12H

27+3I    27

5    8+16    8H

27B

22F

31E    23

22B

31F

4

15I    24    9B

24F

27    24F

6F    4    20B

12H    5    4F

12    4B

2I    27

31B    17B    24F

24F    17B    18F

217 ▲

Use C unless noted otherwise.
Flower centers: 19 I
Small leaves: 24 F

93

# FOLKS

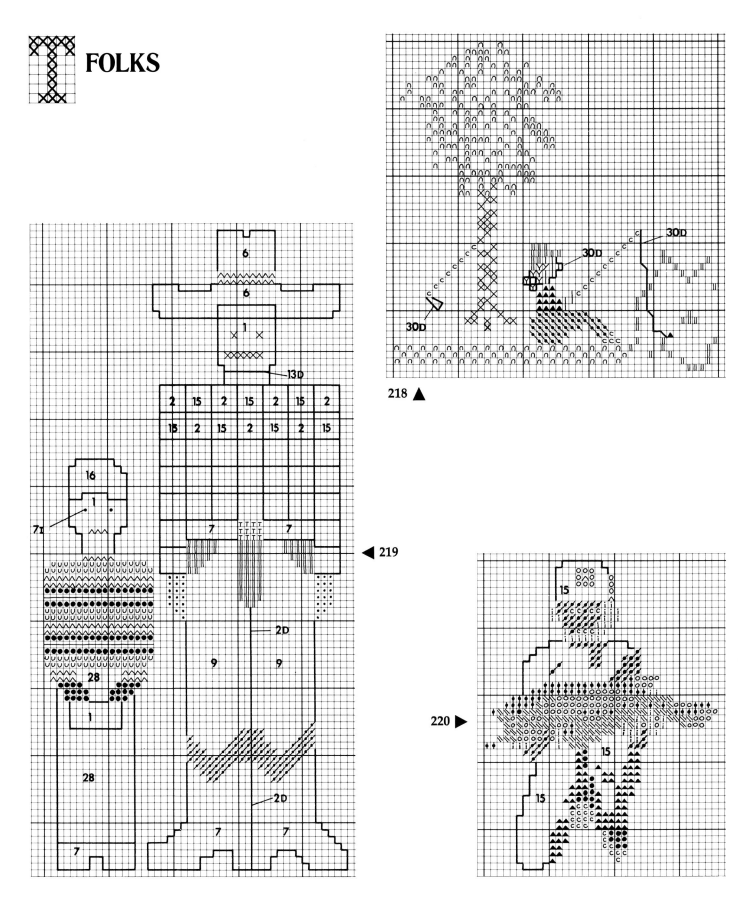

218 ▲

◀ 219

220 ▶

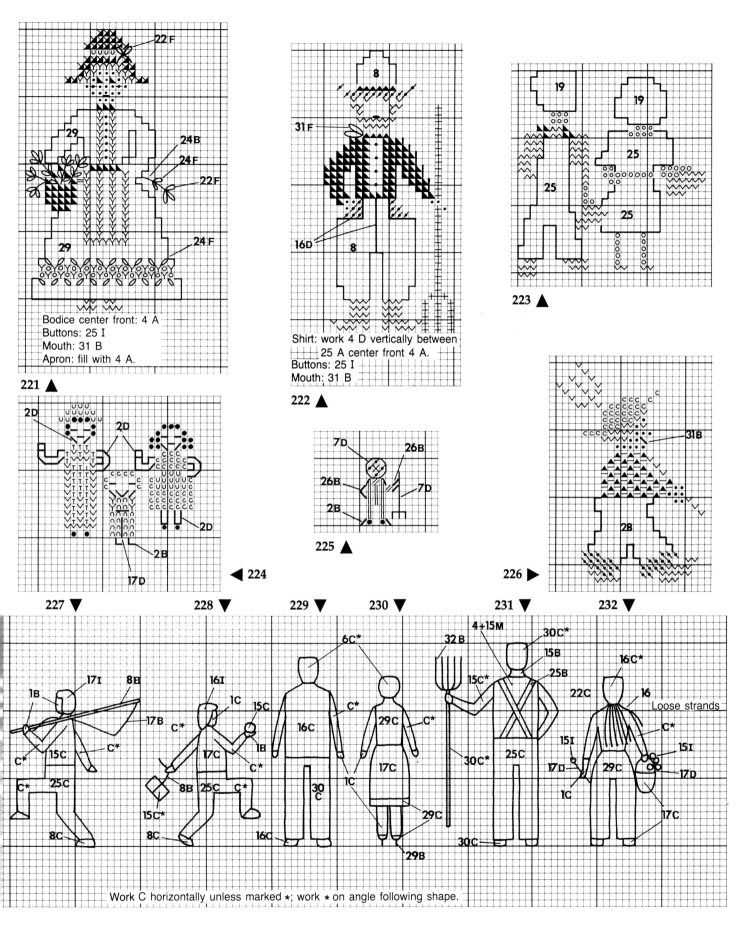

Bodice center front: 4 A
Buttons: 25 I
Mouth: 31 B
Apron: fill with 4 A.

221 ▲

Shirt: work 4 D vertically between
25 A center front 4 A.
Buttons: 25 I
Mouth: 31 B

222 ▲

223 ▲

224 ◄

225 ▲

226 ►

227 ▼  228 ▼  229 ▼  230 ▼  231 ▼  232 ▼

Work C horizontally unless marked *; work * on angle following shape.

95

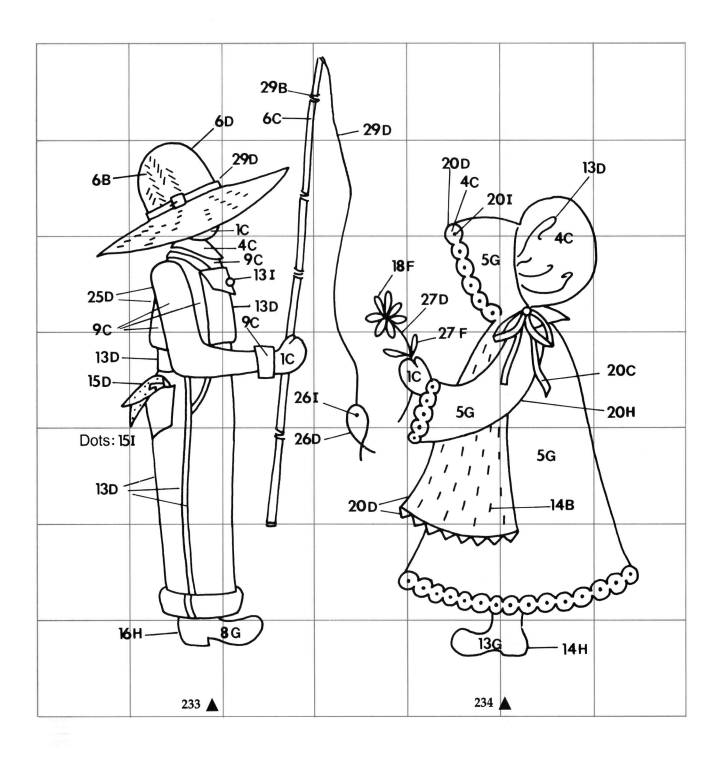

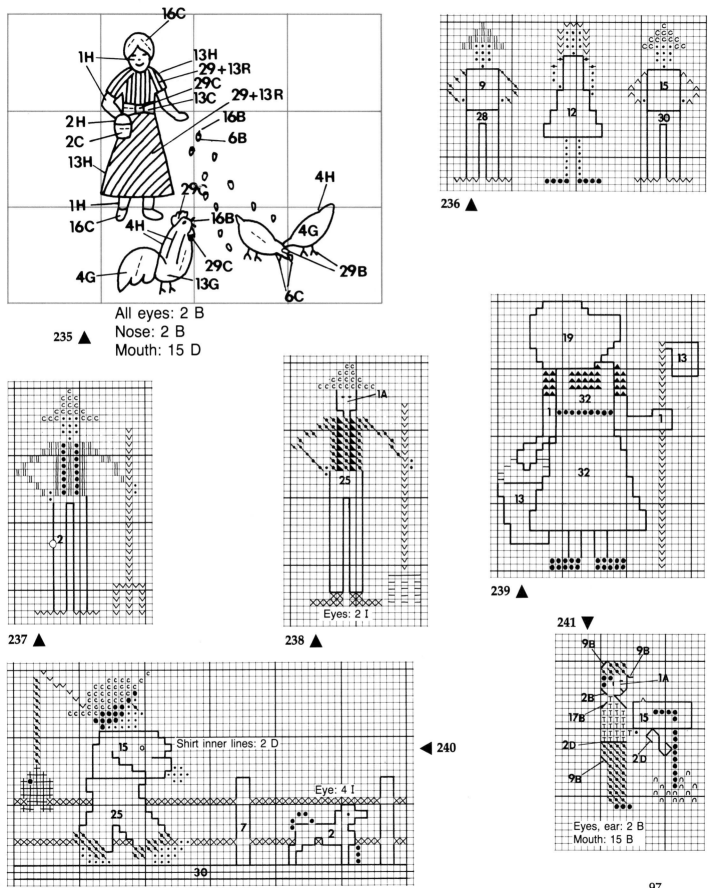

**16C**
**1H**
**13H**
**29+13R**
**29C**
**13C**
**29+13R**
**2H**
**2C**
**16B**
**6B**
**13H**
**4H**
**1H**
**29C**
**16C**
**16B**
**4G**
**4H**
**4G**
**29C**
**29B**
**13G**
**6C**

All eyes: 2 B
Nose: 2 B
Mouth: 15 D

**235 ▲**

**236 ▲**

**9**
**28**
**12**
**15**
**30**

**237 ▲**

**2**

**238 ▲**

c c c
c c c c c c c c
**1A**
**25**
Eyes: 2 I

**239 ▲**

**19**
**13**
**32**
**1**
**32**
**13**

**240 ◄**

Shirt inner lines: 2 D
**15**
**25**
Eye: 4 I
**7**
**2**
**30**

**241 ▼**

**9B**
**9B**
**1A**
**2B**
**17B**
**15**
**2D**
**2D**
**9B**

Eyes, ear: 2 B
Mouth: 15 B

97

# TOOLS AND EQUIPMENT

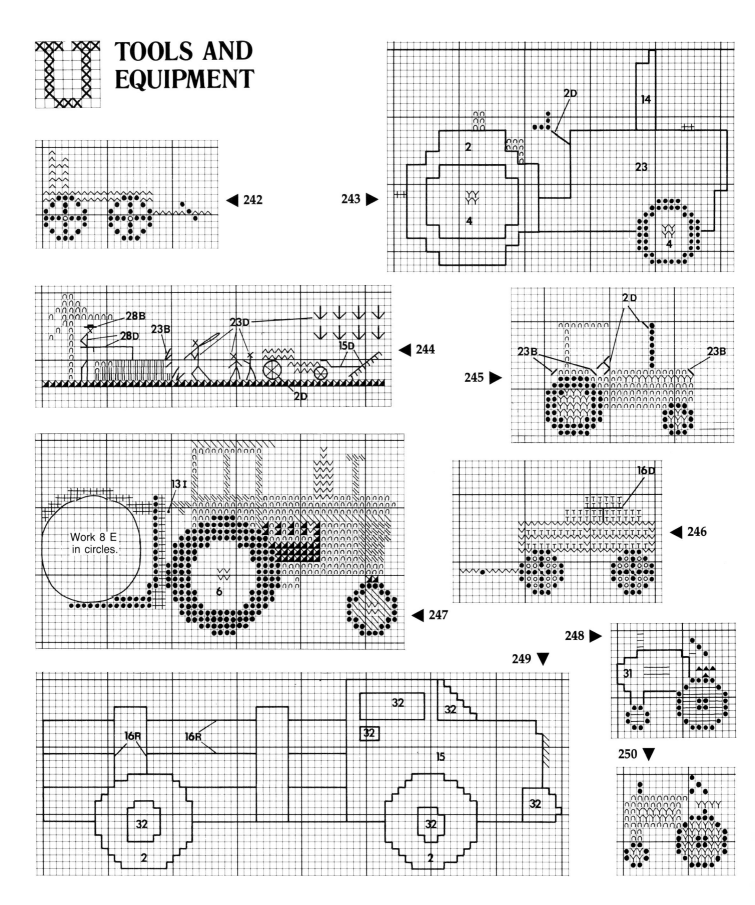

◀ 242

243 ▶

◀ 244

245 ▶

246 ▶

Work 8 E in circles.

◀ 247

248 ▶

249 ▼

250 ▼

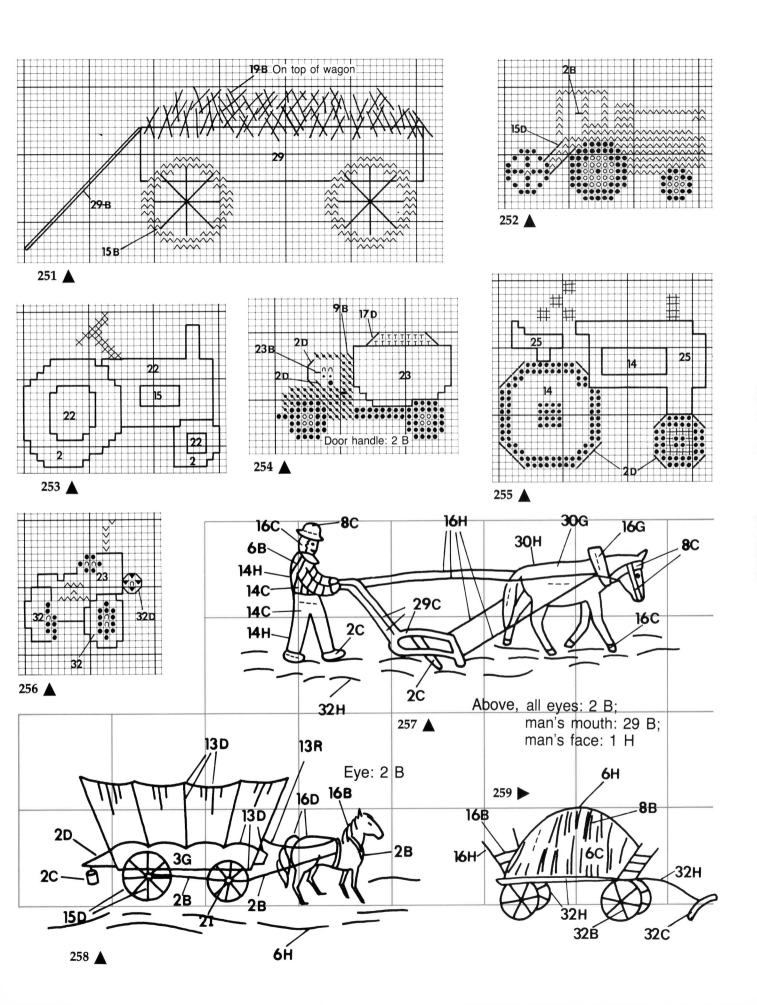

**19 B** On top of wagon

29

29 B

15 B

**251** ▲

**2 B**

15 D

**252** ▲

22

22

15

22

2

22

2

**253** ▲

9 B  17 D

23 B

2 D

2 D

23

Door handle: 2 B

**254** ▲

25

14  25

14

2 D

**255** ▲

23

32  32 D

32

**256** ▲

16 C  8 C

6 B

14 H

14 C

14 C

14 H

16 H  30 G

30 H  16 G

8 C

29 C

2 C

16 C

2 C

32 H

Above, all eyes: 2 B;
man's mouth: 29 B;
man's face: 1 H

**257** ▲

13 D  13 R

Eye: 2 B

**259** ▶

6 H

16 B  8 B

16 D  16 B

13 D

2 D

2 B

3 G

2 C

2 B

15 D

21

2 B

6 H

16 H

16 B

16 H

6 C

32 H

32 H

32 B  32 C

**258** ▲

# TREES

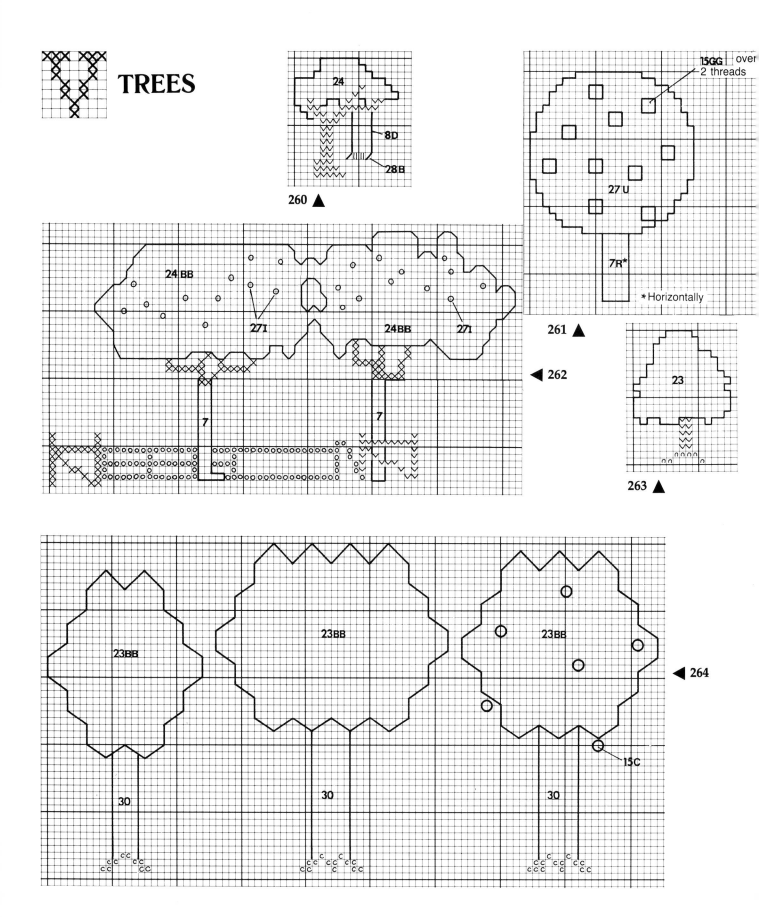

260 ▲

261 ▲

262 ◀

263 ▲

264 ◀

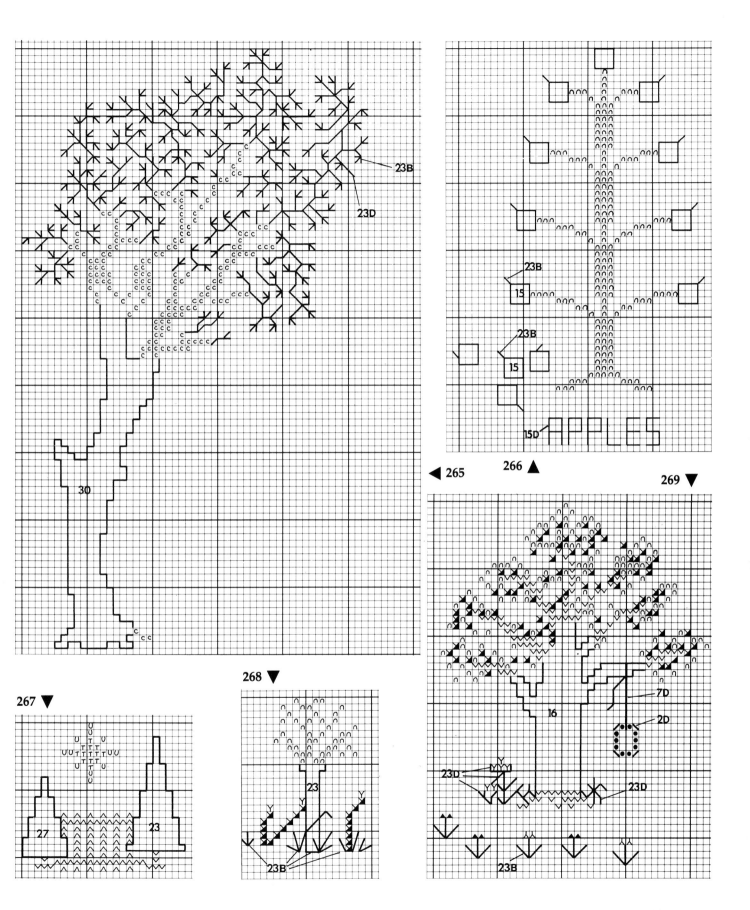

◀ 265

266 ▲

269 ▼

267 ▼

268 ▼

101

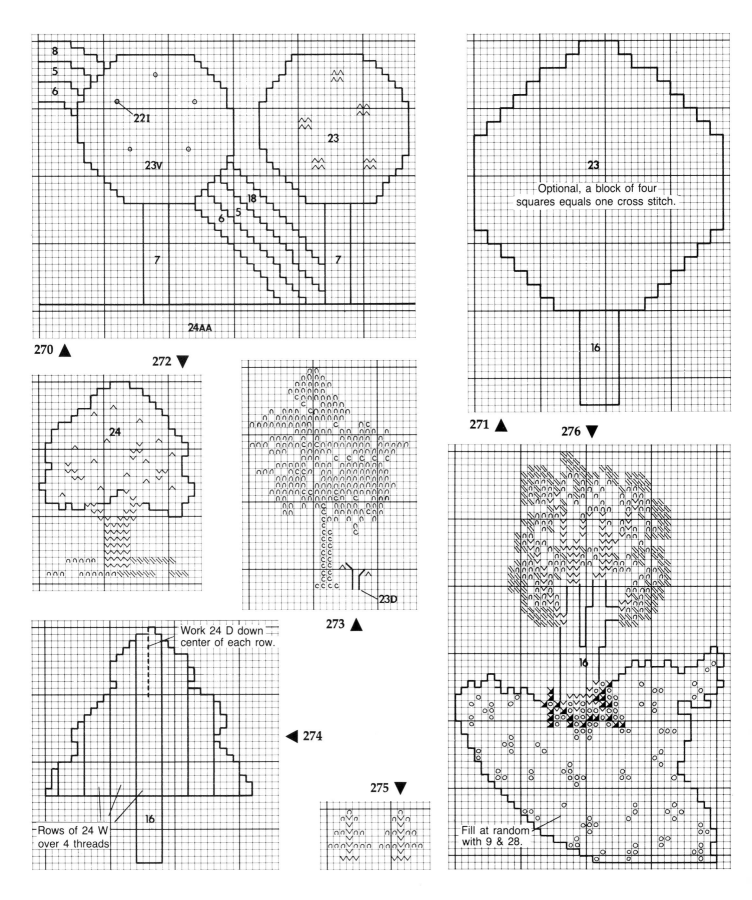

270 ▲

272 ▼

271 ▲

Optional, a block of four squares equals one cross stitch.

273 ▲

274 ◀

Work 24 D down center of each row.

Rows of 24 W over 4 threads

275 ▼

276 ▼

Fill at random with 9 & 28.

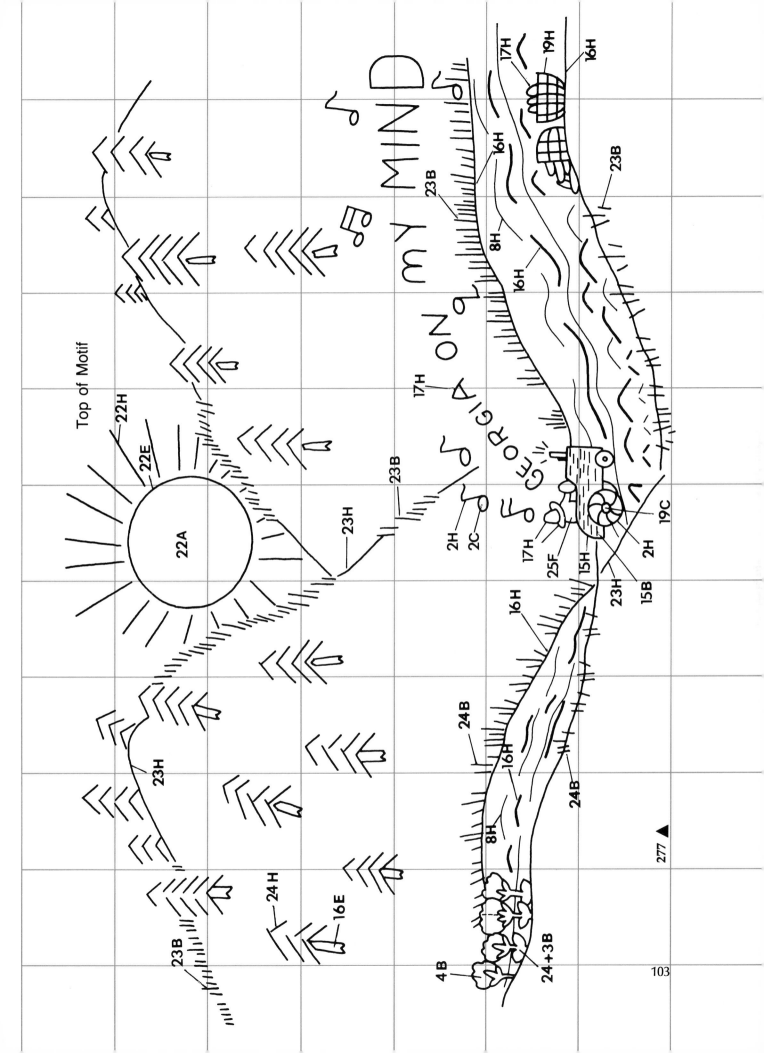

Top of Motif

277 ▲

103

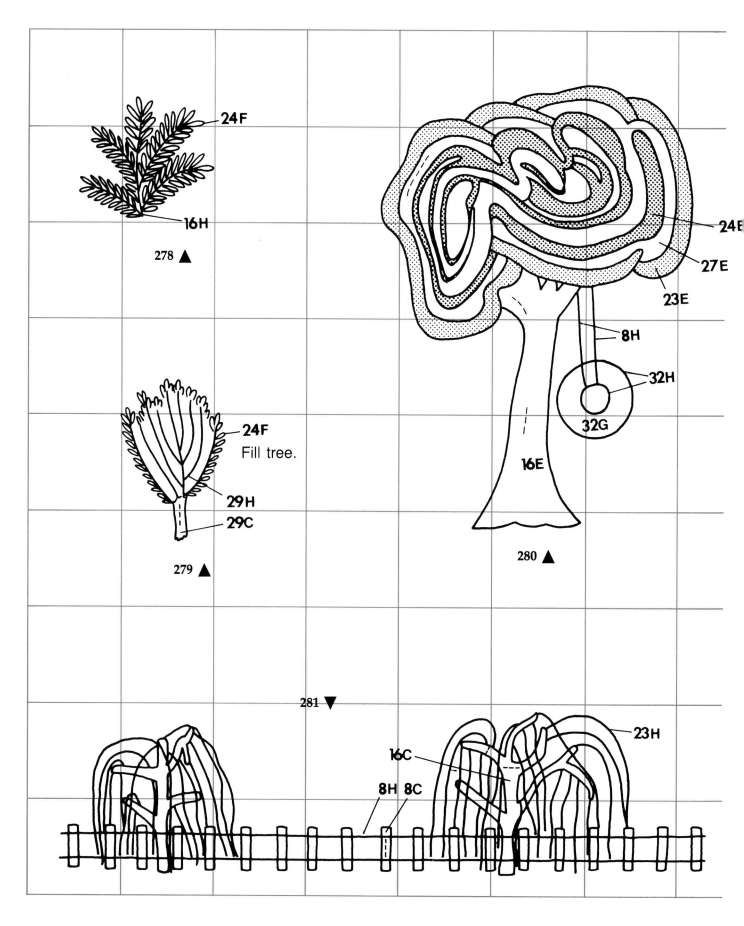

24F

16H

278 ▲

24F

Fill tree.

29H

29C

279 ▲

24E

27E

23E

8H

32H

32G

16E

280 ▲

281 ▼

23H

16C

8H 8C

# MISCELLANEOUS

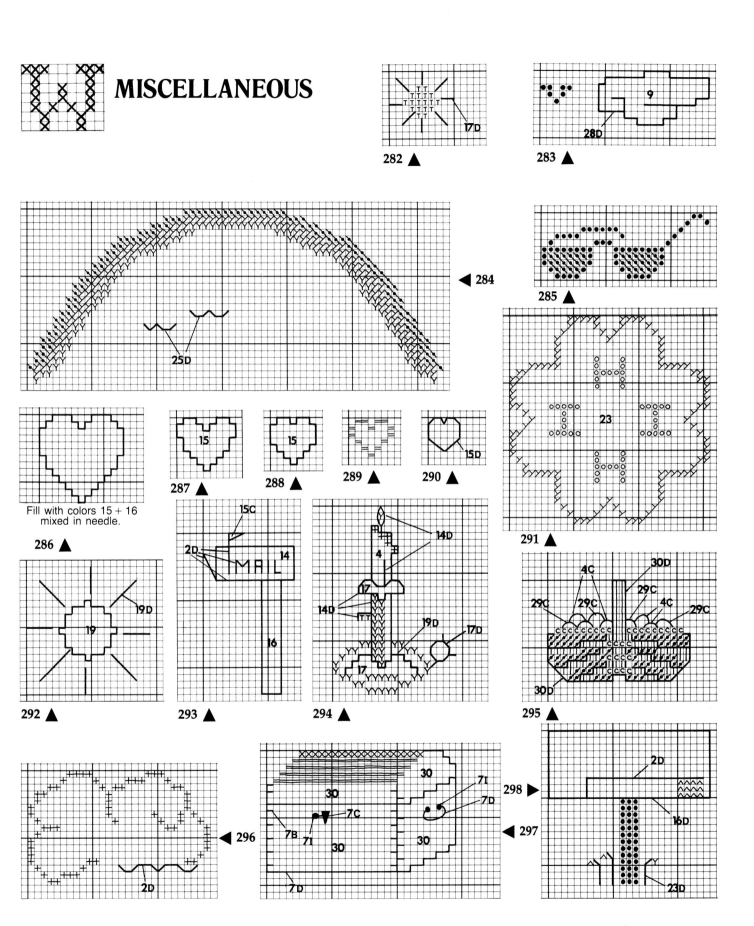

282 ▲

283 ▲

284 ◀

285 ▲

25D

286 ▲

Fill with colors 15 + 16
mixed in needle.

287 ▲

288 ▲

289 ▲

290 ▲

291 ▲

292 ▲

293 ▲

294 ▲

295 ▲

296 ◀

297 ◀

298 ▶

105

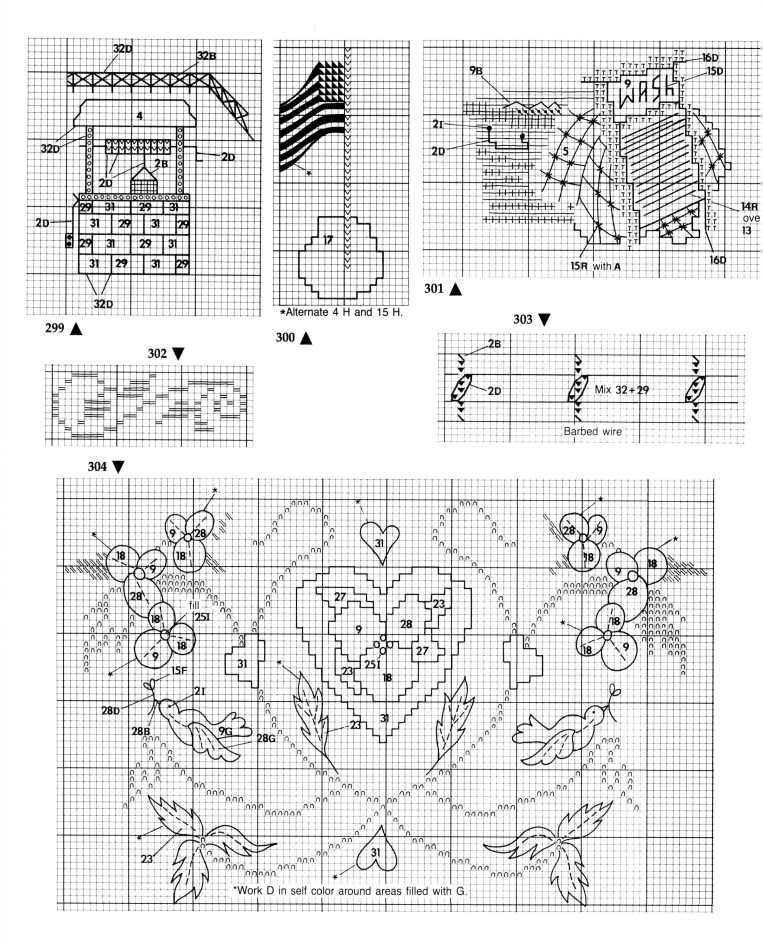

299 ▲

300 ▲

★Alternate 4 H and 15 H.

301 ▲

302 ▼

303 ▼

Mix 32 + 29

Barbed wire

304 ▼

fill
25I

*Work D in self color around areas filled with G.

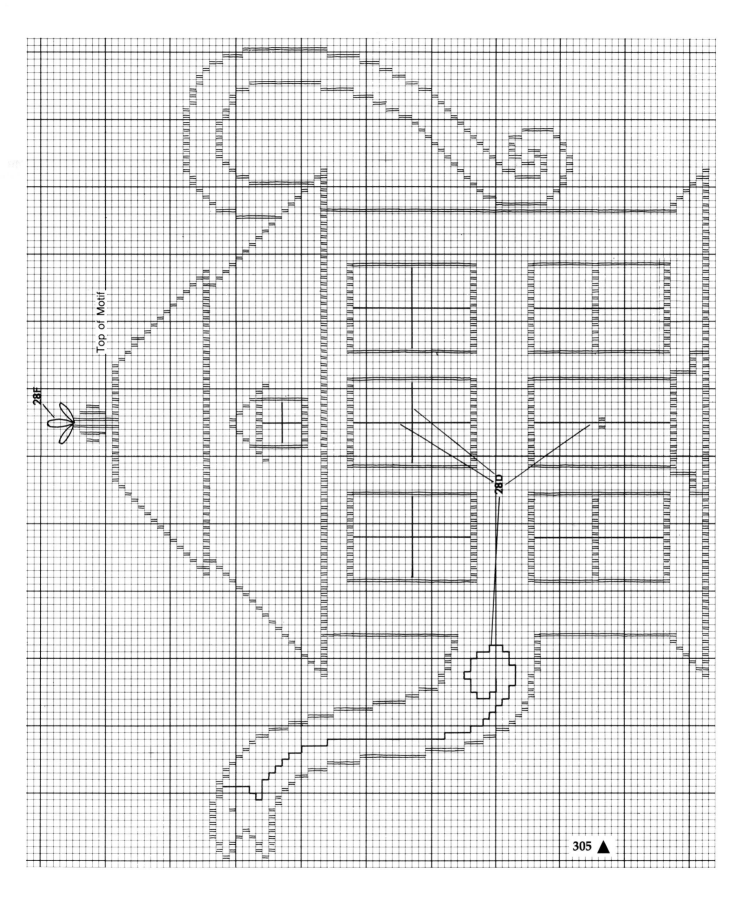

Top of Motif

28F

28D

305 ▲

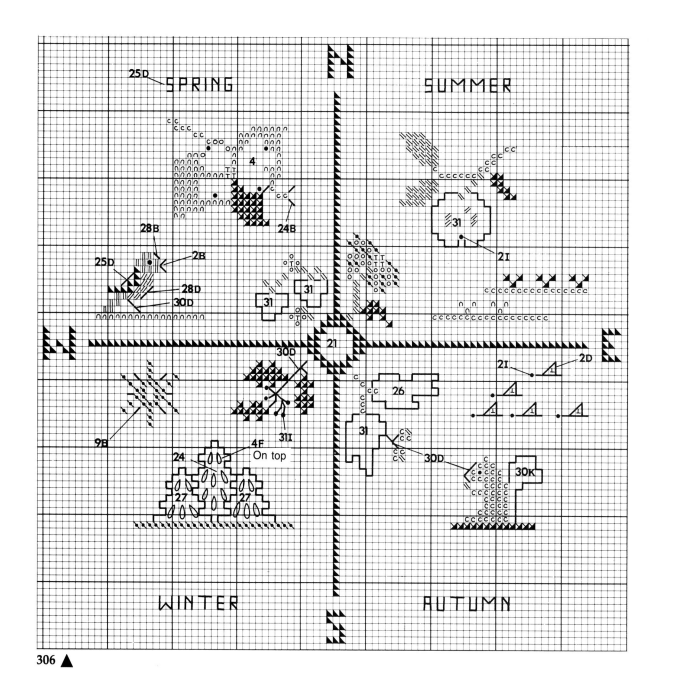

SPRING       SUMMER

25D

28B
2B
25D
28D
30D
24B
4

31
31
31
21
21

30D
9B
31I
24
4F
On top
27   27

26
21   2D
31
30D
30K

WINTER       AUTUMN

306 ▲

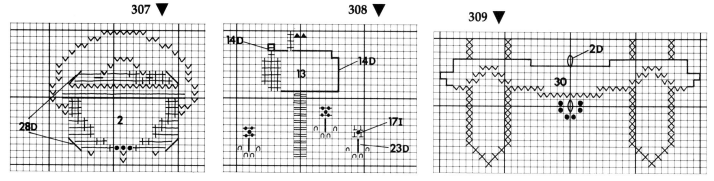

307 ▼

28D
2

308 ▼

14D
14D
13
17I
23D

309 ▼

2D
30

108

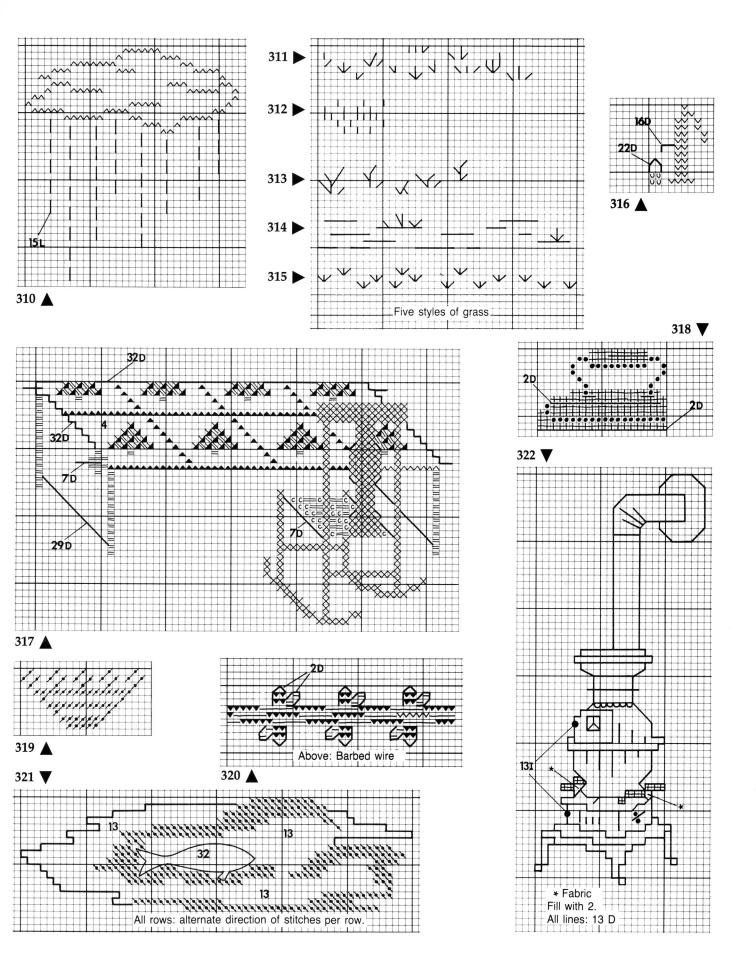

**310** ▲

15L

**311** ▶
**312** ▶
**313** ▶
**314** ▶
**315** ▶

Five styles of grass

**316** ▲

16D
22D

**318** ▼

2D
2D

**322** ▼

**317** ▲

32D
32D
7D
29D
4
7D

**319** ▲

**321** ▼

13
13
32
13

All rows: alternate direction of stitches per row.

**320** ▲

2D

Above: Barbed wire

13I
*
*

* Fabric
Fill with 2.
All lines: 13 D

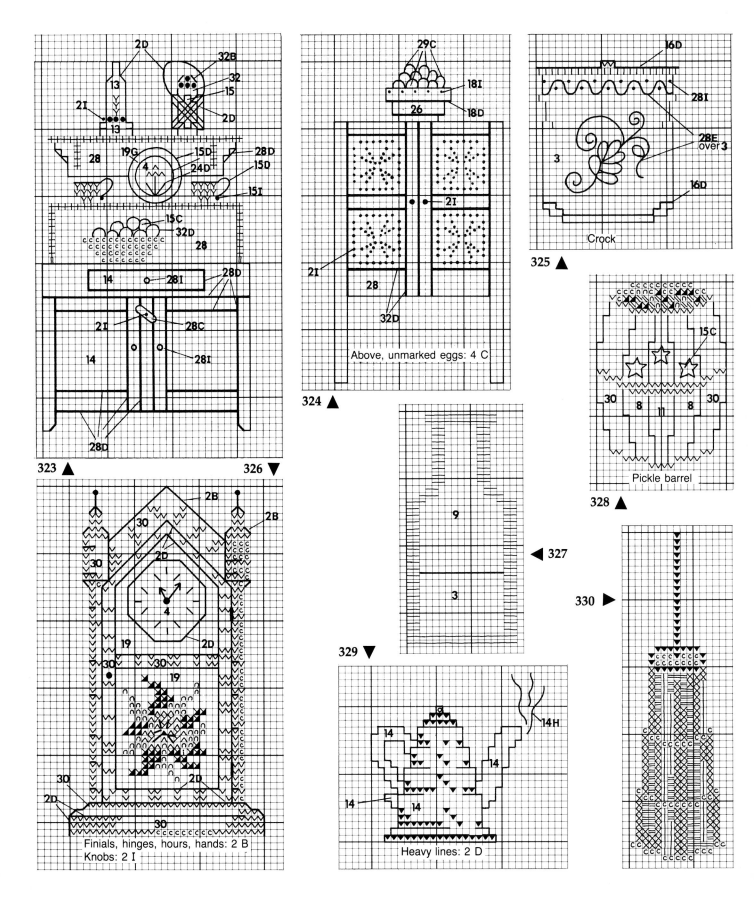

**323** ▲

**324** ▲

Above, unmarked eggs: 4 C

**325** ▲

Crock

**328** ▲

Pickle barrel

**326** ▼

Finials, hinges, hours, hands: 2 B
Knobs: 2 I

**327** ◄

**329** ▼

Heavy lines: 2 D

**330** ►

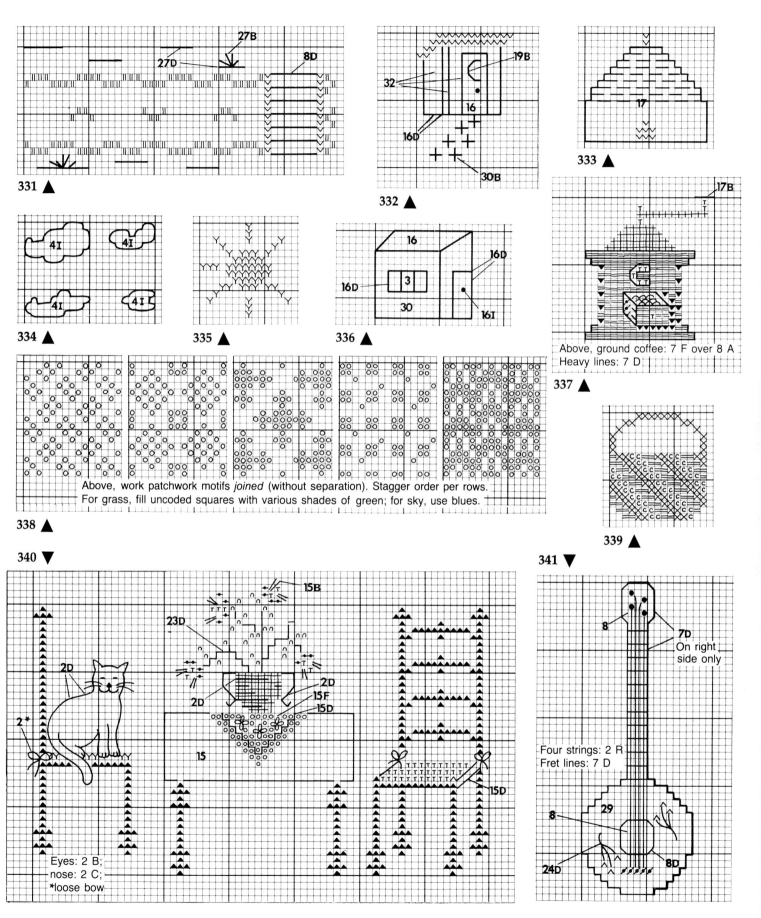

**331** ▲

**332** ▲

**333** ▲

**334** ▲

**335** ▲

**336** ▲

Above, ground coffee: 7 F over 8 A
Heavy lines: 7 D

**337** ▲

Above, work patchwork motifs *joined* (without separation). Stagger order per rows.
For grass, fill uncoded squares with various shades of green; for sky, use blues.

**338** ▲

**339** ▲

**340** ▼

Eyes: 2 B;
nose: 2 C;
*loose bow

**341** ▼

On right
side only

Four strings: 2 R
Fret lines: 7 D

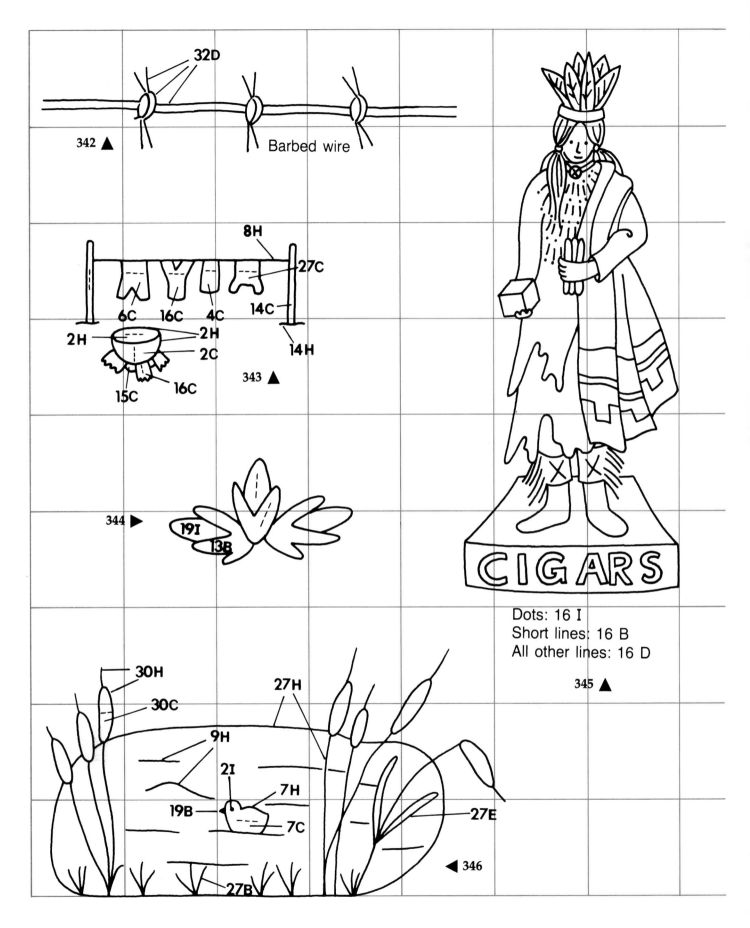

32D

342 ▲    Barbed wire

8H

6C    16C    4C    14C    27C

2H    2H
2C
14H

15C    16C    343 ▲

344 ▶
19I
13B

Dots: 16 I
Short lines: 16 B
All other lines: 16 D

345 ▲

CIGARS

30H
30C

27H

9H

2I

19B    7H
7C

27E

27B    ◀ 346

112

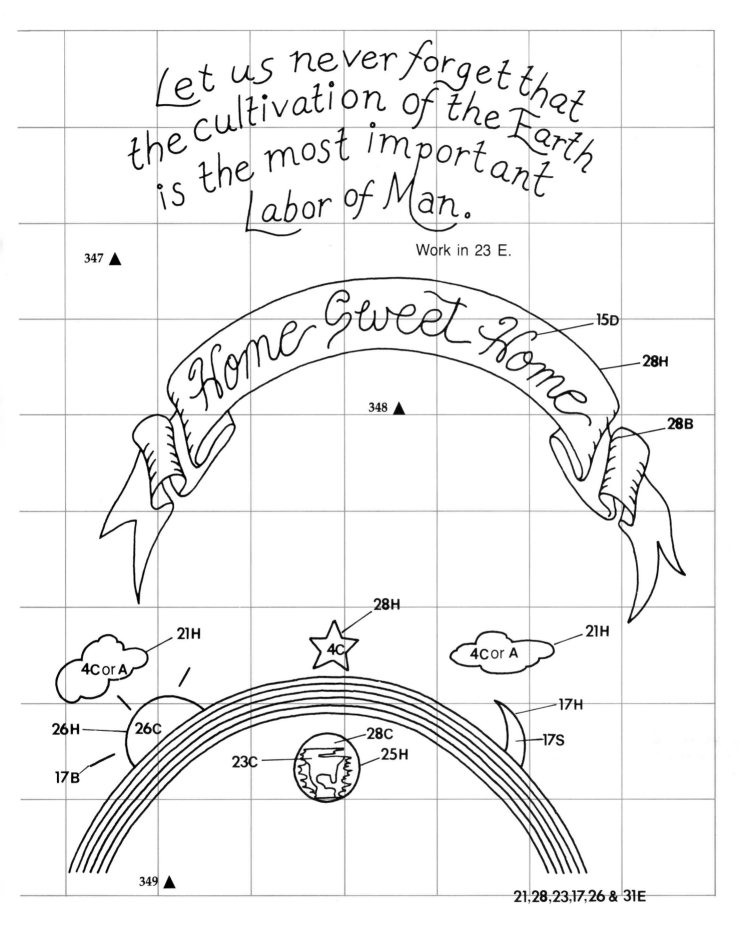

Let us never forget that the cultivation of the Earth is the most important Labor of Man.

Work in 23 E.

347 ▲

Home Sweet Home

15D

28H

348 ▲

28B

28H

4C

21H

4C or A

21H

4C or A

17H

26H

26C

17S

23C

28C

25H

17B

349 ▲

21, 28, 23, 17, 26 & 31E

# HISTORICAL MOTIFS

350 ▼

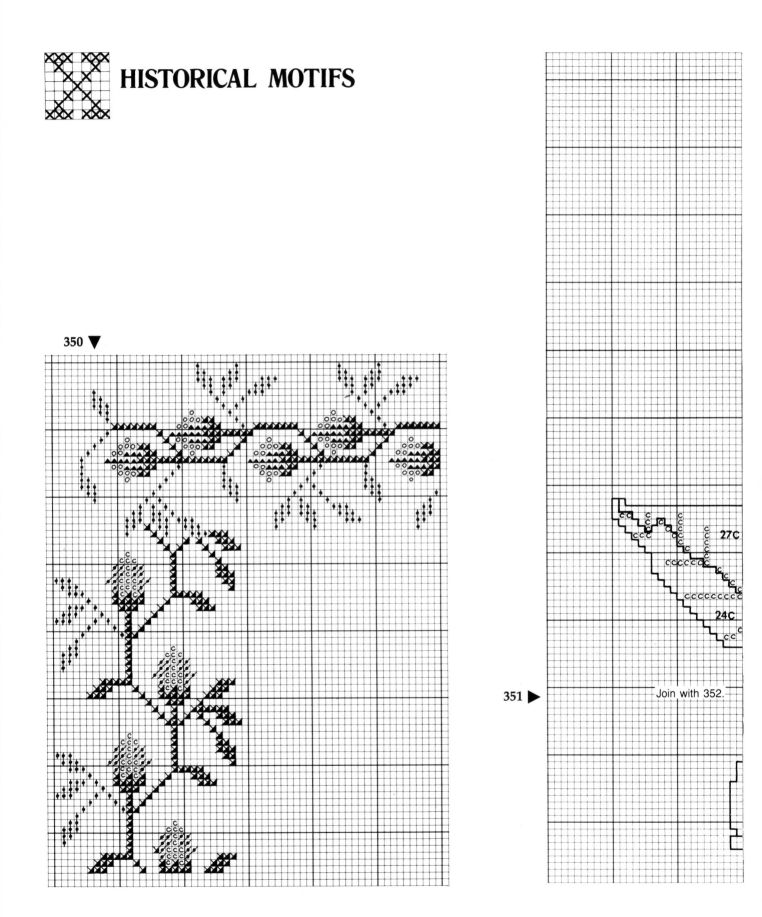

351 ▶

27C

24C

Join with 352.

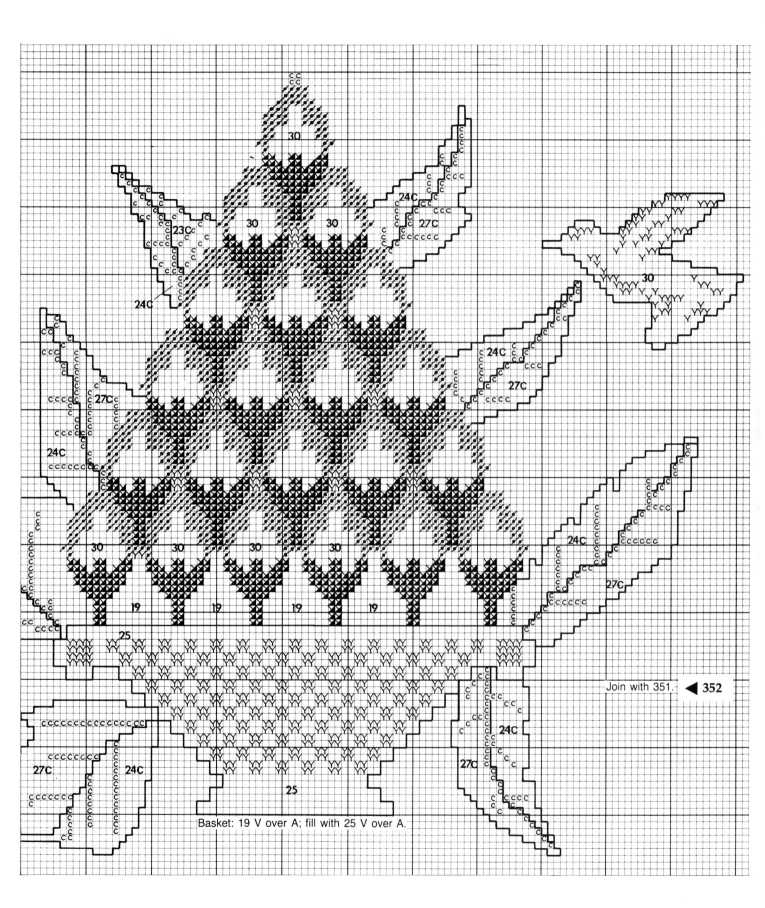

Join with 351. ◄ **352**

Basket: 19 V over A; fill with 25 V over A.

115

353 ▲

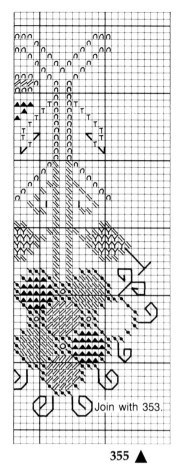

355 ▲

Join with 353.

356 ▼

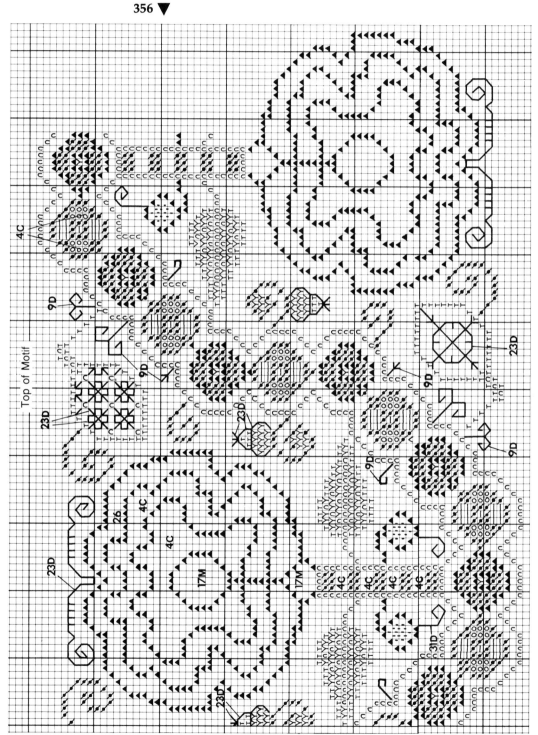

Top of Motif

4C

9D

23D

23D

4C

2b

4C

17M

17M

9D

9D

23D

9D

4C 4C 4C 4C 4C

31D

23D

Top of Motif

27D

27D

27D

27D

27D

Continue small top and bottom borders full length of motif.

27C

27C

4C

4C

17

4C

4C

27C

27C

17

31D

27D

26C

4C

4C

3ID

3ID

27D

27D

17D

24

17B

31D

4C 9C

9C 4C

4C 9C 4C

25D (also inner lines)

9D

31D

3ID

27D

3ID

27D

31D

24D

27D

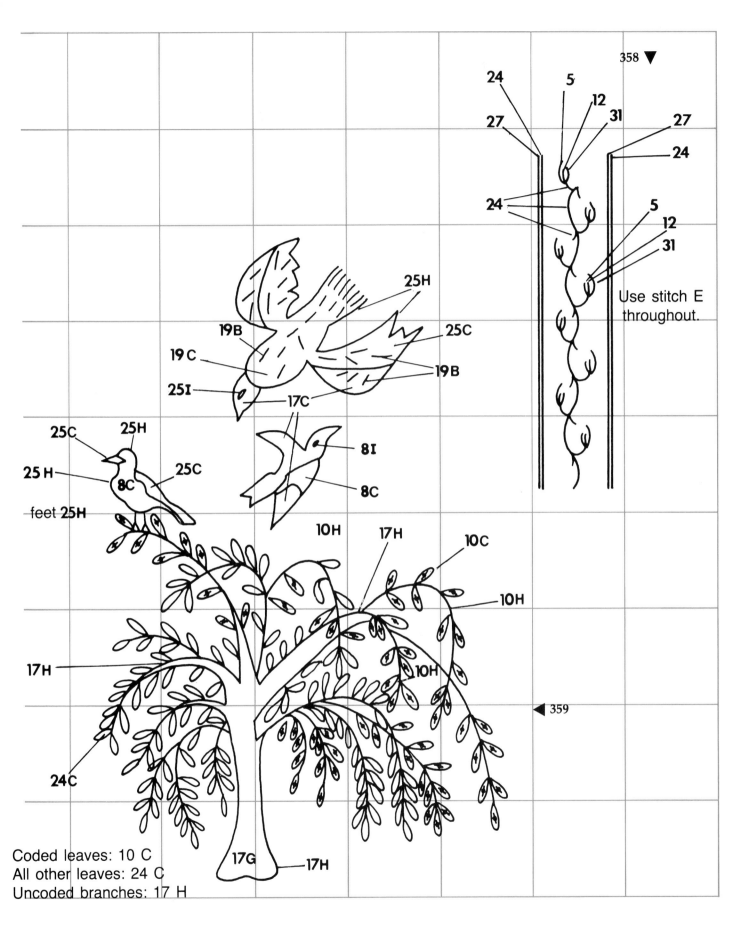

358 ▼

24
5
12
31
27
27
24

24

5
12
31

Use stitch E throughout.

25H

19B

19 C

25C

251

17C

19B

81

8C

8C

25C
25H

25 H
25C

25 H
8C

feet 25H

10H

17H

10C

10H

10H

17H

359

24C

17G

17H

Coded leaves: 10 C
All other leaves: 24 C
Uncoded branches: 17 H

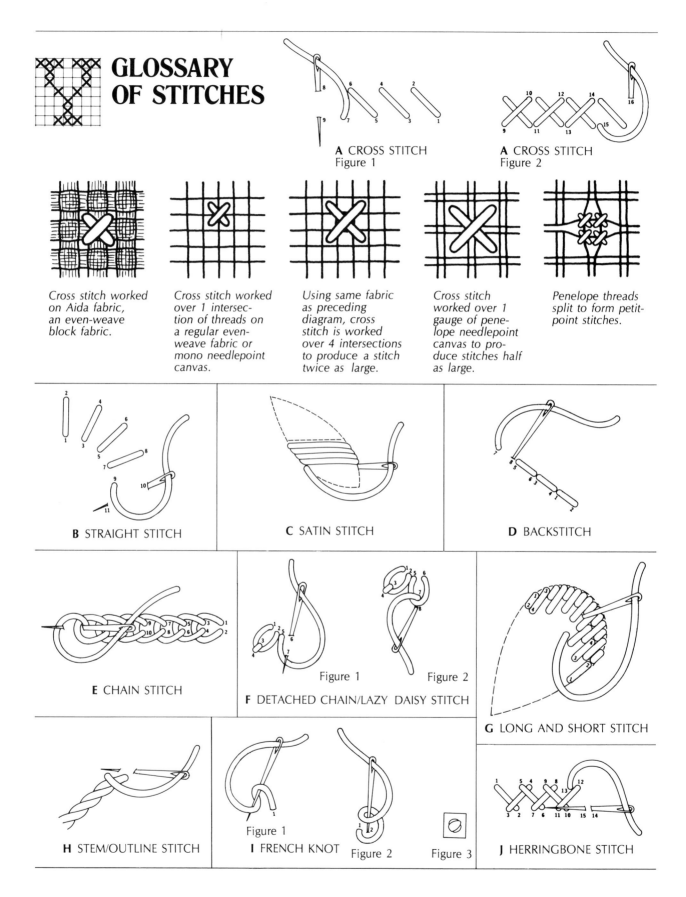

# GLOSSARY OF STITCHES

**A** CROSS STITCH
Figure 1

**A** CROSS STITCH
Figure 2

Cross stitch worked on Aida fabric, an even-weave block fabric.

Cross stitch worked over 1 intersection of threads on a regular even-weave fabric or mono needlepoint canvas.

Using same fabric as preceding diagram, cross stitch is worked over 4 intersections to produce a stitch twice as large.

Cross stitch worked over 1 gauge of penelope needlepoint canvas to produce stitches half as large.

Penelope threads split to form petit-point stitches.

**B** STRAIGHT STITCH

**C** SATIN STITCH

**D** BACKSTITCH

**E** CHAIN STITCH

**F** DETACHED CHAIN/LAZY DAISY STITCH
Figure 1    Figure 2

**G** LONG AND SHORT STITCH

**H** STEM/OUTLINE STITCH

**I** FRENCH KNOT
Figure 1    Figure 2    Figure 3

**J** HERRINGBONE STITCH

120

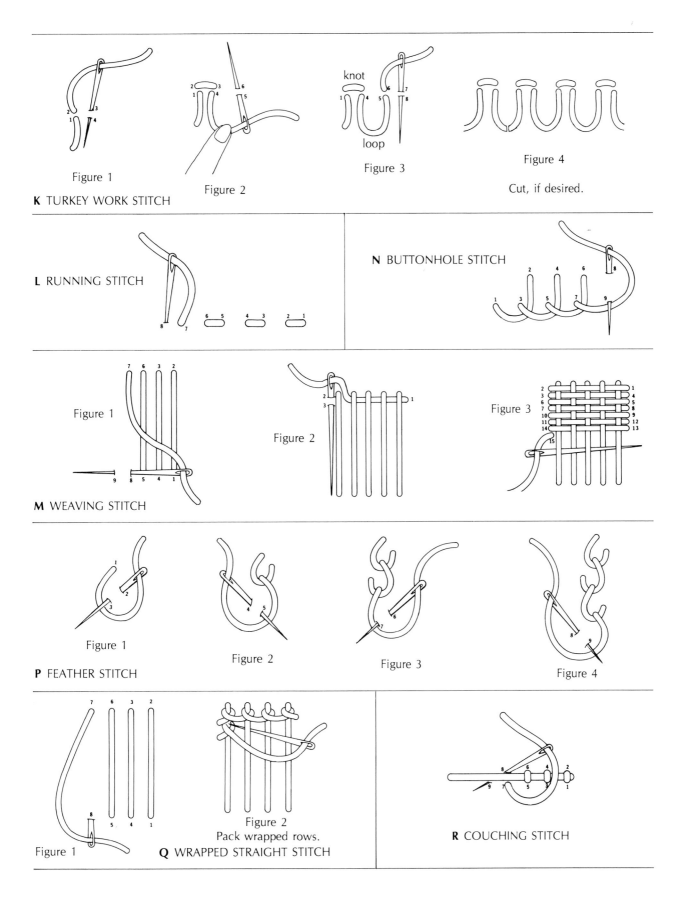

Figure 1

Figure 2

knot

loop

Figure 3

Figure 4

Cut, if desired.

**K** TURKEY WORK STITCH

**L** RUNNING STITCH

**N** BUTTONHOLE STITCH

Figure 1

Figure 2

Figure 3

**M** WEAVING STITCH

Figure 1

Figure 2

Figure 3

Figure 4

**P** FEATHER STITCH

Figure 1

Figure 2
Pack wrapped rows.
**Q** WRAPPED STRAIGHT STITCH

**R** COUCHING STITCH

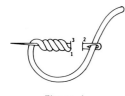

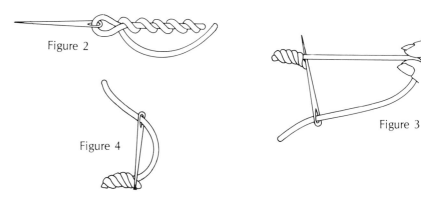

Figure 2

Figure 3

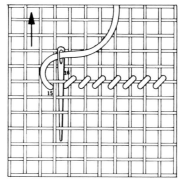

Figure 4

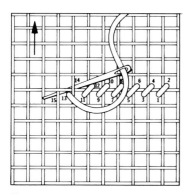

Figure 1

Number of wraps can vary.

**S** BULLION KNOT

---

**T** TENT STITCHES

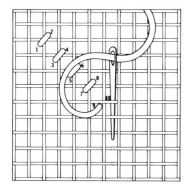

Figure 1

Work row from right to left.

CONTINENTAL STITCH

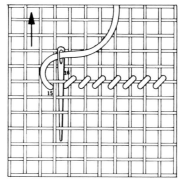

Figure 2

Finish last stitch.

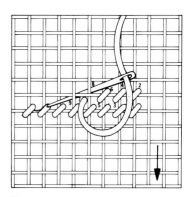

Figure 3

Turn canvas upside-down on alternate rows; work new row right to left.

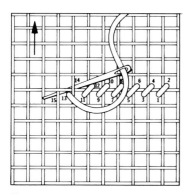

Figure 1

BASKETWEAVE STITCH

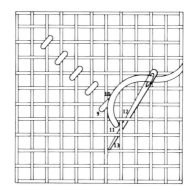

Figure 2

Begin new row.

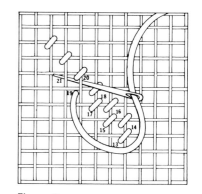

Figure 3

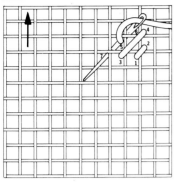

Figure 1

**U** MOSAIC STITCH

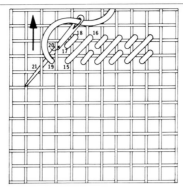

Figure 2

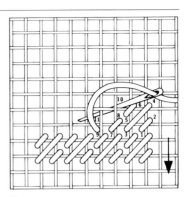

Figure 3
Turn canvas upside-down on
alternate rows.

Figure 1

**V** UPRIGHT CROSS STITCH

Figure 2

Figure 3

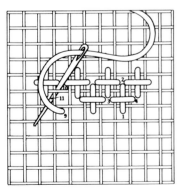

Figure 4

123

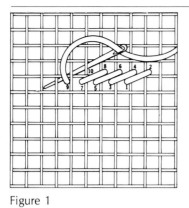

Figure 1

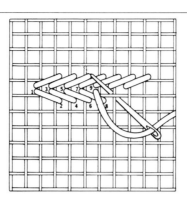

Figure 2

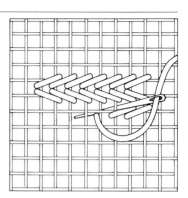

Figure 3

**W** KALEM STITCH

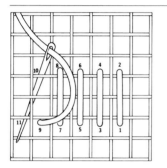

**X** STRAIGHT GOBELIN STITCH

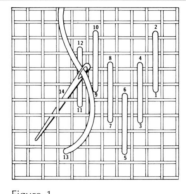

Figure 1

**Y** FLORENTINE STITCH

Typical variation of peaks and valleys; number of stitches per repeat may also vary.

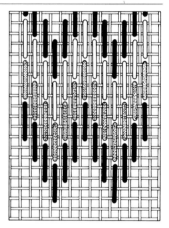

Figure 2

Number of color rows may vary.

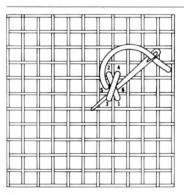

Figure 1

Work row from right to left.

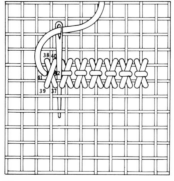

Figure 2

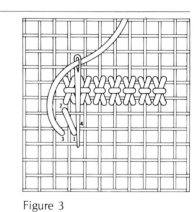
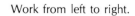

Figure 3

Work from left to right.

**Z** OBLONG CROSS WITH BACKSTITCH

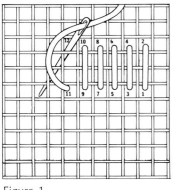

Figure 1

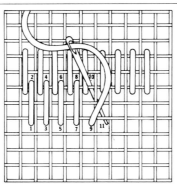

Figure 2 Position new stitches consistently to right or left.

**AA** ENCROACHING STRAIGHT GOBELIN STITCH

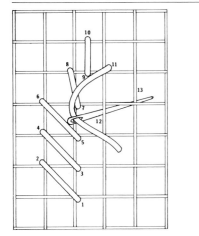

Figure 1

**BB** LEAF STITCH

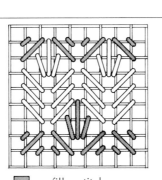

 = filler stitches

Figure 2

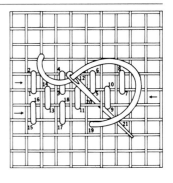

**CC** BRICK STITCH

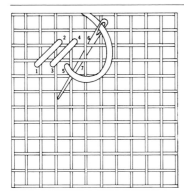

Figure 1

Figure 2

Figure 3

**DD** BYZANTINE STITCH

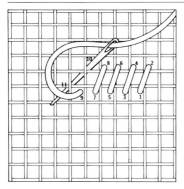

Figure 1

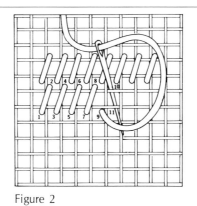

Figure 2

**EE** SLANTED GOBELIN STITCH

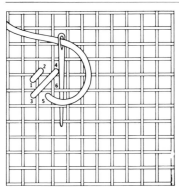

Figure 1

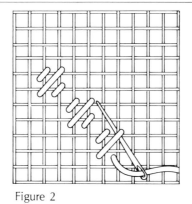

Figure 2

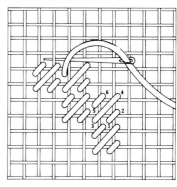

Figure 3

**FF** DIAGONAL MOSAIC STITCH

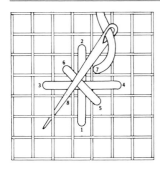

**GG** DOUBLE CROSS STITCH

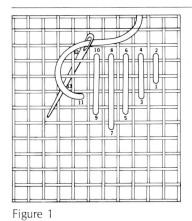

Figure 1

**HH** TRIANGLE STITCH

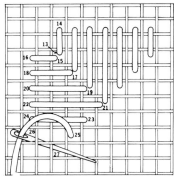

Figure 2

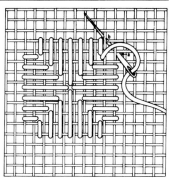

Figure 3

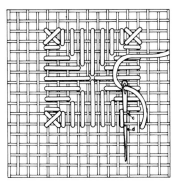

Figure 4

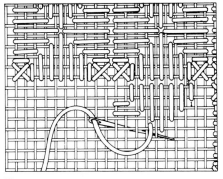

Figure 5

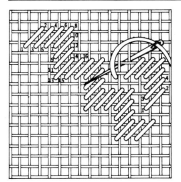

Figure 1
Work long stitches.

**II** JACQUARD STITCH

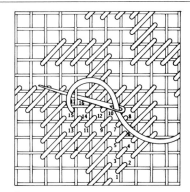

Figure 2
Work filler stitches.

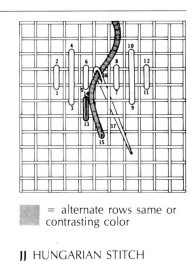

 = alternate rows same or contrasting color

**JJ** HUNGARIAN STITCH

## BIBLIOGRAPHY

Bath, Virginia Churchill. *NEEDLEWORK IN AMERICA.*
New York: The Viking Press, 1979.

Fawdry, Marguerite, and Deborah Brown. *THE BOOK OF SAMPLERS.*
London: Cameron & Tayleur Books, Ltd., 1980.

Kay, Dorothea. *EMBROIDERED SAMPLERS.*
New York: Charles Scribner's Sons, 1979.

Krueger, Glee F. *A GALLERY OF AMERICAN SAMPLERS.*
The Theodore H. Kapnek Collection. New York: E. P. Dutton in association with the Museum of American Folk Art.

Lopo, Ana G., and Bruce W. Murphy. *THE SAMPLER BOOK.*
New York: Crown Publishers, Inc., 1978.

Sebba, Anne. *SAMPLERS: FIVE CENTURIES OF A GENTLE CRAFT.*
New York: Thames and Hudson, Inc., 1979.

---

## SOURCES

The following individuals and enterprises contributed their resources to the projects presented in this book: JOAN TOGGITT, LTD., 246 Fifth Avenue, New York, New York, (Herta, Klostern, Aida, Gardasee, Floba, Davosa, Hardanger, Lugana, Linda, Gerda, Belfast, and waste canvases); D.M.C. CORP., 107 Trumbull Street, Elizabeth, New Jersey, (cotton floss, pearl cotton, A Broder, Retors A Broder, Persian, and tapestry wool yarns); C.M. OFFRAY AND SONS, INC., 261 Madison Avenue, New York, New York, (grosgrain and satin ribbons); MRS. BARBARA MANNING, THE ATTIC ANTIQUES, Birmingham, Alabama; MRS. GRACE CARTEE, THE CORNER CUPBOARD, Cullman, Alabama; BONNE HANNA, HANNA ANTIQUE MALL, Birmingham, Alabama; JEANIE PERRYMAN, PLAYFAIR, INC., Birmingham, Alabama.

---

## COUNTRY SAMPLERS

EDITOR: Grace Hodges
PRODUCTION EDITOR: Annette Thompson
EDITORIAL ASSISTANT: Patty E. Howdon
DESIGN: Viola Andrycich
PHOTO STYLIST: Linda M. Stewart
PHOTOGRAPHY: Mac Jamieson
PRODUCTION MANAGER: Jerry Higdon

**Front Jacket Cover,** *cross stitch and embroidery on ivory-color Hardanger fabric using the following motifs: 13 (reduced and transposed to embroidery), 33, 58, 63, 67, 96, 98, 101, 118, 212 (reduced), 312 (enlarged).*

**Back Jacket Cover,** *cross stitch with embroidery details on ivory-color Hardanger using the following motifs: 118, 171, 174, 182, 192, 221, 222, 295.*